Fulltiming

FULLTIMING

AN INTRODUCTION TO FULL-TIME RVING

Newly Revised

GAYLORD MAXWELL

LIFE ON WHEELS, INC.

First Printing: May, 1991
Second Printing: May, 1992
Third Printing: July, 1994 (Revised)
Fourth Printing: July, 1998

ISBN: 0-9741961-0-X

CIP data available upon request.

Published by Life on Wheels, Inc.
P.O. Box 9755
Moscow, Idaho 83843
www.lifeonwheels.com

Cover and Interior Design by Robert S. Tinnon Design
Cover photograph taken near Deary, Idaho, by the author
Production services by Rena J. Copperman

Printed by Patterson Printing Co., Benton Harbor MI 49022

Additional copies may be obtained from

Life on Wheels, Inc.
P.O. Box 9755
Moscow, Idaho 83843

Please send $12.95 per copy plus $3.00 shipping and handling.

To Margie . . .

My wife
My co-pilot
My companion
My friend
My sweetheart

. . . for over half a century

Contents

Preface

Before I read any book, especially those written by "authorities on the subject," I like to know something about those authorities. I want to know what their credentials are and see evidence that they are truly qualified to give advice about whatever the subject may be. I feel that I owe that same courtesy to readers of this book.

Assuming that you would appreciate some assurance that my credentials are sufficient to position me to "advise," I offer the following information about my life.

My first career was as a teacher, but after seventeen years of trying, with varying degrees of success, to make U.S. history exciting for high school and college students, I opted for a new vocation. An interest in camping and RVing led me into that field, and, for two decades, I did my best to encourage and teach people to camp and travel while I earned a living selling them recreational vehicles and camping equipment.

Apparently I succumbed to my own sales pitch because nearly two dozen years ago, I sold the business and embraced a lifestyle that required most of our time to be spent RVing—a lifestyle that fit perfectly with my former secondary, now primary, occupation as a writer for Trailer Life publications and presenting seminars on the RV lifestyle at RV shows.

After "retiring" from the lecture circuit in 1994, I revived a concept I had developed on paper to offer RVing classes at colleges. A chapter on the history and current status of that project—Life on Wheels—will be discussed later in this book.

As with many RVers, we started camping in tents when we were young. Our first experience as a family with RVs (they weren't called RVs then) was when we rented a 16-foot trailer in 1954 for a trip to Yosemite. Later we used fold-down trailers most of the years when our three kids were growing up. Then came the truck camper phase—even a BIG 10-footer. After some travel trailer experiences, we tried a fifth-wheel, and in 1972 got our first motorhome. In the years since, there have been twelve others, and I expect there will be at least one more.

In all, Margie and I have traveled some half-million miles in motorhomes, and, although we are not fulltimers (we have a home in northern Idaho), for the past twenty-three years, our typical year has been from three to five months at home and seven to nine months in a motorhome. If we added the months up, I'm sure we've spent fifteen years in motorhomes.

We've traveled in all forty-eight of the contiguous states, several Canadian provinces, and have taken several extended trips into Mexico. We've stayed in elegant resorts, and we've boondocked in Arizona deserts; we've marveled at Nature's wonders at Yellowstone, and we've enjoyed man's wonders at Silver Dollar City; we've visited relatives and friends in their homes while we stayed in ours, and we've taken some of them (grandkids and our parents) with us at various times; we've made long trips over long periods of time without breakdowns, and we've had trips where one thing after another plagued us (including burning up a two-month-old 40-foot motorhome); we've visited hundreds of interesting historical sites ranging from those where incredible events took place (e.g., Gettysburg) to those that are barely remembered in history books (e.g., Hornitos, in the gold rush country of California); we've made friends in million-dollar motorhomes and others in two-thousand-dollar rigs. We've seen a lot; there's no question about that, but we don't claim to have seen it all. And during all those adventures, I've learned. In fact, I consider myself a student of

RVing. I feel that I know enough to pass some of it on to others. I gladly learned and I will gladly teach.

What follows is a blend of what I have seen, felt, and done combined with what we have learned from others. I hope these views will be useful to readers, especially those who are considering fulltiming and have questions about life on the road.

I refer to this book as a "Dick and Jane" book for those who are in the very preliminary stages of considering full-time RVing. I have tried to pose most of the questions that occur to people who are thinking about that lifestyle and offered not so much direct answers as some options. The various personal experiences I relate or refer to are provided, not to instruct the reader to do things my way, but to give reference points for self-direction. That approach is used because of my personal wariness and reluctance to pay much heed to people who try to tell me how I should do things. In my judgment, what these people do is tell me what they prefer, the way they do things, and that might not be what I or someone else should do at all. I prefer to have several options from which I may choose and modify to suit my particular needs and likes.

The reality is that there is no more a single way to do full-time RVing than there is to live a "regular life" in a house somewhere. A common factor is that RV fulltimers are on wheels, but the variations from that point on are as diverse as people anywhere. Wise people will inform themselves as much as possible about the many options available, do some experimenting and investigating, and choose a path suited to their needs and circumstances. RV fulltiming is very democratic; you can have it your way because what you make of it is largely up to you.

Good luck! I hope we meet down the road.

Acknowledgments

Although the information in this book draws primarily from over four decades of experience as an RVer, I must give credit to the original source of much of the knowledge that I claim: our fellow RVers. Like a sponge, I soak up every "how-to" lecture, every "where-to" recommendation, every "what-to" suggestion, every yarn, every story I read in RV magazines and books and file away for recall when I need it. Much recollecting was done to fill the following pages. Thank you, RV friends.

I would also like to thank my friends at TL Enterprises who have been instrumental in my career as a writer for TL publications for over thirty years. Bill Estes, Bob Livingston, Barbara Leonard, Sherry McBride, and Maxye Henry have corrected my mistakes, polished my phrasing, and have subtly guided me over the hundreds of articles I have written for *MotorHome, Trailer Life,* and *RV Business* magazines. And I especially would like to thank Mike Schneider, who has served in many capacities at TL where he has greatly assisted me. Thank you, my TL friends.

But my biggest "thank you" goes to Margie, my partner for over half a century, who has "gone along with the program," regardless of where it took us—sometimes with interminable miles, appalling roads, wretched weather, crappy campgrounds, and all-too-frequent breakdowns. She has always tried to look at the good side of whatever the objective was and enjoyed the happy endings, of which there have been so many.

Introduction

A secret—sometimes not so secret—desire of many Americans is to move into a trailer or motorhome and just roam around the country, staying where they wish as long as they wish, seeing all of the wonderful scenery, enjoying the natural beauty of our country, fishing, filming, painting, just looking, or doing whatever their "thing" is without concern for schedules or clocks or what other people want—in short, a desire to be free.

Perhaps it's the heritage passed on to us by Daniel Boone, Kit Carson, the forty-niners, and the countless thousands of our restless ancestors. Included are the Joe Smiths and Bill Joneses who didn't achieve anything noble or great but, like those who did famous deeds, couldn't hack the restrictions imposed by living in one place. They knew there were roads to be taken, bends in the river to follow, mountains to climb, deserts to cross, sights to be seen, and riches to be gained. Like an itch, the yearning to go places and see things has to be scratched, and the only way to do that is to go. For the fulltimer, the itch is permanent and requires continuous scratching.

Hordes of today's Americans do just that. Studies indicate that there are approximately a million people now living full time in their RVs. My personal feeling is that this estimate is too conservative. Unfortunately, since counting "birds on the wing" is difficult, we have no precise number. Suffice it to say that there are lots of fulltimers, and the number is growing. In fact, if only half the people who talk about it actually take up the lifestyle, we'll need a lot of new facilities to accommodate them in the years to come.

Perhaps before we get too involved with the subject of fulltiming, we ought to determine just what we include in the term. Strictly defined, the words *full-time RVing* mean living 365 days a year in an RV. Anything less is not fulltiming.

Many RVers fall into a category that we call *extended-timers*—those who spend a great deal of time (like six months a year) on the road. They return to homes for the rest of the time. They have roots, a fact that differentiates them from the true fulltimer.

However, since many of the needs, experiences, joys, and rewards of extended timing are similar to those of fulltiming, much of what follows is pertinent to that category of RVers. Indeed, the extended-timing period is often the schooling period for fulltiming. RVers who "test the waters" for six- to eight-month periods learn the lessons that will guide them in their preparations for fulltiming.

So, for my purposes in this book, the information is directed toward those who are interested in spending extended periods of time on the road as well as those who are preparing for the whole nine yards.

CHAPTER ONE

Would I Be a Successful Fulltimer?

One of the first questions that people who are considering fulltiming should ask is: Am I the kind of person who would fit the lifestyle? Going from living a "regular" or "normal" life in a house with all the trappings that go with it to living in an RV is a big change in one's life. It's equal to going from single to married, from childless to parenthood, from life with kids to empty-nesting. It has the potential to enable practitioners to experience a life filled with pleasure and contentment; it can also, unfortunately, lead to unhappiness and discontent. It is definitely an issue that deserves as much attention and education as possible before a decision is made.

I'm sure that most people who even think about going fulltiming must have some of the characteristics that encourage people to take up a life on wheels; otherwise, they wouldn't even think about it or would be almost repelled by the idea. Usually fulltimers come from the ranks of already experienced RVers. However, it seems that an increasing number of people I talk to are thinking of starting at zero—totally inexperienced about RVing. They are the ones who need to ask themselves very seriously, Am I suited for the full-timing lifestyle?

It would be great if people could take aptitude tests to find out whether or not they are suited for fulltiming. Although no truly scientific test exists, I developed the Maxwell Full-timing Aptitude Test a decade ago and hundreds of people have taken it. It's fun to take and test results do provide some indication of a person's mental makeup as it pertains to factors that are involved in full-time RVing.

The twenty-five items on the multiple-choice test on pages 121 to 126 all have some connection with fulltiming. To give yourself clues about some of your attitudes on how you want to live your life, take the test now before you read any further. It won't positively tell you what you should do, but it can indicate the direction you are leaning toward. Score your test results and then read Chapter Two, "What Are Fulltimers Like?" for some explanations.

What Are Fulltimers Like?

Now that you have taken the Maxwell Full-timing Aptitude Test, you should compare your responses with some findings that most observers of fulltimers generally have concluded.

There are at least seven common characteristics of a successful fulltimer: dissatisfaction, curiosity, a sense of adventure, gregariousness, daring, patience, and compatibility.

Dissatisfaction

If you are completely satisfied with the kind of life you are living, then there's probably no reason to change to something drastically different and risk the unknown. If you get up very happy, spend your day pleased with your activities and circumstances, and go to bed happy, then you should ask yourself, "Why would I want to give this up?" You definitely need a convincing answer before you take the far-reaching step that takes one from "regular living" to full-time RVing. In short, you should be dissatisfied with the way you are living if you are considering making a big change in your life.

Being dissatisfied doesn't necessarily mean being terribly unhappy, but it does mean that you are looking for something new and different. You want change. You want something more exciting, more attractive, something that gives more satisfaction. You have an itch to go and do and see.

People contemplating full-time RVing usually fit the dissatisfied cat-egory. They would like to replace whatever it is that is lacking in their lives with something that will fulfill them. Naturally, they have dreams about the joys of life on the road. However, it should be pointed out that sometimes fulltimer-wannabes' perceptions of the lifestyle are over-glamorized and oversimplified. The consequences can be that the real-ity doesn't match the ideal, and disillusionment results. Just as with most endeavors, attitudes and expectations must reasonably coincide with the realities if success is to be achieved. Fulltiming has some negative aspects—make no mistake about that. People who can't adjust to or accept these negatives will probably find that fulltiming, rather than being a dream come true, is a nightmare.

Those thinking about becoming fulltimers should possess a number of special qualities that will enhance their experiences with the lifestyle. These including the following:

Curiosity

In most cases, show me a fulltimer and I'll show you a person who has multi-interests—someone who likes to explore, to see, and do new things. Fulltimers usually like to visit those places marked on maps as special—those that indicate destinations such as public parks, his-torical sites, and other attractions open to the public. In fact, they spend a lot of time looking at atlases, planning for new adventures down the road. Stories they hear others tell about "fabulous places" they've been to set them to itching. They know they haven't seen it all and never can, but they like to try.

Sense of Adventure

Like their footloose-and-fancy-free predecessors, the pioneers that opened America up, fulltimers want to find out what is around the bend, what is over the hill, what is down the road—so they go for it. They want to see and experience new things. A good reason for them to take a road is simply that they've never been on it before.

Gregariousness

Most fulltimers are people oriented; they mix with neighbors in campgrounds and parks wherever they are. They are people who like people. Formal introductions aren't necessary for neighborly chatting. Unlike city people who cast their eyes downward when they meet other folks on sidewalks, RV people who meet in campgrounds almost invariably smile and greet each other. Parties, especially the impromptu kind, are a crucial part of the RV social life. Often those parties are simply a few couples bringing their chairs, and perhaps refreshments, to gather under someone's awning for chitchat and story swapping.

Many fulltimers find their circle of friends grows more and more to include other fulltimers. By keeping in contact via e-mail and cell phones, they arrange to meet throughout the year at various events and places. They become involved in each other's families and share joys and grief. It's amazing how many of them stick by each other when troubles arise, especially health problems.

Daring

It takes more than a little nerve to be a full-time RVer. In the first place, just attempting it requires considerable spirit. To tackle mountain roads, city traffic, and other challenging conditions on our highways at the wheel of a monstrous multi-ton rig—be it trailer or motorhome—is not a job for wimps. Simply because fulltiming often involves heading into the unknown, practitioners need be blessed more than a little with courage.

Patience

Impatience simply doesn't square with the RV lifestyle, which is basically a "take-it-easy" mode. Anyone who has driven a rig up Vail Pass in Colorado, or White Bird in Idaho, or Burgess Junction Pass ("Oh-My-God Hill") in Wyoming, or any of the other long, steep grades that one encounters in mountains knows how important it is to be able to relax while "thundering" along wide-open at twenty-seven miles per hour.

A reality of the RV lifestyle is that we park very close to each other—in some parks as little as six feet apart. We share common facilities, so consideration for one's fellow man becomes particularly important. And when the snoring you hear at midnight is coming through your open bedroom window via your neighbor's open bedroom window, the challenge to love your fellow man can become serious. But most fulltimers understand the need for patience and consideration for their RV neighbors.

Compatibility

Quite simply, there isn't much fighting room in an RV, so traveling companions must like each other to make it through the days and nights in spaces that often don't exceed 300 square feet of floor space. Full-time couples are together 24 hours a day, 7 days a week, 30 or 31 days a month, 365 days a year—always within shouting distance, often within striking distance of each other! So, if they don't really like each other, the odds of enjoying fulltiming are remote. Of course, getting a larger RV is a partial solution. There's more fighting room in a 30-footer than there is in a 20-footer (Margie and I are now up to 39 feet!).

Summary

Of course, there are other characteristics that describe many fulltimers, but these are the most identifiable ones. One doesn't necessarily have to fit a mold that includes all of them, but I think it would be difficult to be a happy, successful fulltimer without having any of them.

Who Doesn't Fit?

Who does not fit the full-timer mold? Actually, there are all kinds of people fulltiming, even some old grouches who I suspect have taken up life on the road primarily because they can't get along with neighbors at a fixed place. Of course, they don't get along with other RVers either, but they're easy to move away from. An anomaly that I see in boondock areas is the occasional trailer parked a half-mile from all other rigs. I can only assume that the occupants don't want to be around other folks. Obviously, they aren't gregarious.

One kind of person who definitely doesn't fit the full-timer lifestyle is the "old poop"—the guy who doesn't do anything, doesn't think anything, and doesn't want to deviate from a comfortable state of lethargy. He can usually be found in his living room in front of his TV watching whatever happens to come on—or just dozing his days and years away.

CHAPTER THREE

What Must I Give Up to Be a Fulltimer?

Several basic aspects of "regular living" will be given up if you become a full-time RVer. Included are:

A Fixed Place

Most people are associated with a *place*, that is, they have an address where anyone who cares to investigate can find them. Whether it is a street number, rural route box, or an apartment number, it is a definite place, and the mail carrier, UPS delivery person, the police officer, or any person in the world who can read a map can locate you or send something to you. The fact that many people refer to where they live as "my place" is a clue as to how people feel about their own space on this planet. We often in referring to someone associate them with a city, street, part of town, or where their place is located in the country.

But when you take up fulltiming, you give up that fixed place, and people no longer associate you with a geographical spot. It can be confusing to people when their friends or relatives aren't settled in a place. For example, we have three kids whom we have phoned regularly in our travels. In fact, for the past twenty-plus years, we've always called them every weekend. Their first question is always, "Where are you?" (I secretly grin with delight at those questions and tell myself that I'm getting even with them for all the times I've wondered where *they* were. Fulltiming provides many good opportunities to get even with your children for some of the worries they put you through).

Actually, most fulltimers have a sense of "place," but it's simply their RV. It is their home and wherever it is parked is their place.

The Familiar

Another element one gives up for fulltiming is the *familiar*: things, people, and places. People, especially those who have lived in the same place for many years, face exactly the same sights from the time the wake up until they go to bed. The contents of the house, the same yard with the same shrubs, the trees, the neighbors' houses, the neighbors themselves, the streets, the stores—it's all the same day after day, year after year.

When you take up fulltiming, all that changes. Although your RV will be familiar, where it is parked usually won't be. You may be in the mountains one day and in a desert the next. We find it interesting to awaken in the morning and the first thought that pops to mind is, "Where are we?" On occasion, I've had to push the blind back to see outside to get the answer. "Oh, gee, the KOA in Sioux Falls," or "Wow, there's a deer standing over there by the edge of the river!" There's always something new and different to start the day.

Routines

We're all accustomed to regular routines in our daily lives. We get up in the morning and generally follow very closely the same actions every day of our lives—the same place at the table, the same route to work, the same job, and the same chores when we get home. All that changes when you go fulltiming. Admittedly, you get into some other routines, but you do a lot of things differently because you are in new surroundings and have more opportunities to go in various directions.

Chores

You give up a lot of the chores you've become accustomed to when you hit the road: no more lawn to mow, no shrubs to trim, no leaves to rake, no house painting, no house to vacuum and dust, no garage to tidy up. Sure, there's housekeeping to do, but there's quite a difference between cleaning a big 300-square-foot motorhome and a 3,000-square-foot house. Of course, there's a downside—you get some new chores. On days that you travel, that means windshield washing and debugging the front of the truck or motorhome. The maintenance of the vehicles becomes major, especially with a motorhome, which has so many gadgets and gizmos that need to be tended. But the amount of choredoing in an RV is far less than that required for maintaining a "regular" home.

Expenses

As a full-time RVer, you give up a lot of expenses. It is possible as a fulltimer to live on a lot less than it costs for the normal household to live a "regular" life. However, you will note that I don't say definitely that fulltiming is less expensive that "regular' living. Sure, you give up a lot of expenses—property taxes, big utility bills, house maintenance, and so forth—but you also pick up some new ones. Campground fees,

higher fuel bills, and maintenance of your rig will have to be reck-
oned with. However, fulltiming can be much less expensive than living in a regular home because the major expenses can be controlled.
More information on that can be found in Chapter Eighteen, "How
Much Does Fulltiming Cost?"

CHAPTER FOUR

What Do I Get from Fulltiming?

I've asked hundreds of fulltimers what they get from fulltiming, and the answers are pretty much the same. Chief among those responses are the following:

A New Freedom

Fulltimers are in agreement that the main advantage they gain from the lifestyle they have chosen is *freedom*—freedom from the restrictions and obligations that a normal life in a house imposes. It's freedom from routine, freedom from the myriad chores of maintaining a property, freedom from being tied down, and freedom from boredom. You get the opportunity to choose where you'll be, when you'll be there, and what you will do when you get there. You'll be rid of the grooves that keep you on the straight and narrow and the time and opportunities to direct your own life in both the big things and the small. This new freedom does not mean taking on a primitive lifestyle. It's not like camping. Modern RVs can be as plush and comfortable as you wish (or can afford), with many of the amenities of a regular home. Most newer, full-timer rigs have comfortable furniture, a completely equipped kitchen with microwave, blender, built-in coffee maker, icemaker, side-by-side refrigerator-freezer, and filtered water. Some even boast washer-dryers, dishwashers, and trash compactors. Nearly all have two TVs, stereo, VHS/DVD—complete entertainment systems. Many have good accommodations for computers and related equipment.

In short, one does not have to give up comfort to become a full-time RVer. In fact, it's a lifestyle that gives people more time to enjoy the comfort features of their homes.

Opportunities

Fulltimers are regularly exposed to new opportunities to participate in activities that were not readily available to them in "regular" life. For example, many RV parks, particularly those that cater to snowbirds, have facilities and instruction in arts and crafts, dancing, sports, physical fitness programs, cultural events, and all kinds of classes that aren't readily available to people who live in houses. In parks, participants have these offerings practically next door and at modest or no expense. It's all a part of the package when you pay for space.

We have friends who took art lessons one winter and both became quite proficient. Indeed, one even sells some of her paintings. Other friends took up square dancing in the park where they were staying and have progressed through the various levels until they are now quite expert.

Because fulltimers are regularly exposed to new sights, places, and activities, it isn't unusual for most of them to take advantage of some of the opportunities they are exposed to. Also, the fact that they are always meeting new people who have different interests and skills tends to stimulate new interests. Sometimes those new friends are willing and able to provide some instruction, too.

Education

To repeat a cliché, travel is broadening. I've often said, "Show me some-one who has fulltimed for ten years, and I'll show you someone who deserves a Ph.D. in general education." You can't help but learn as you travel. Geography lessons learned on the road are the best kind. Many fulltimers eventually sample the entire United States and know firsthand what the terrain is like, the various climates, what people do to make a living, what crops are grown where, the names of rivers and moun-tains, and much more. I get a kick out of hearing a group of people who have been fulltiming for a long time discuss places they've been. Con-versations are spotted with questions like, "Were you ever at . . . ?" Or, "Did you ever see . . . ?" Frequently the response is, "Yeah, we were there in . . ." And so reminiscing about their adventures is a kind of lesson for listen-ers who haven't been there.

Many fulltimers have a fascination with our history and like to learn stories about the past in the places they visit. History is much more meaningful if you are standing at Kitty Hawk reading the marker des-ignating the spot where the Wright brothers flew, or the battlefield at Gettysburg peering into the rocks at Devil's Den, where Northern troops fired at charging Southerners, or at the reconstructed fort at Fort Clatsop, where Lewis and Clark spent a miserable winter in Oregon. Thousands of such sites lure history buffs, and these visitors generally leave with a better knowledge of our history and a greater appreciation for our country.

Fulltimers have many opportunities to learn about science and cul-ture by visiting museums. For example, our space program makes a lot more sense after one has visited Cape Canaveral in Florida—par-ticularly if they are fortunate enough to witness a launch as we were. Huntsville, Alabama, where most of our rockets were developed, also has

a space museum and provides an excellent, brief history of space explo-
ration and our part in it. The NASA Space Center in Houston rounds
out the "big three" for very realistic lessons on our space history.

The Cowboy Hall of Fame in Oklahoma City is devoted to the mem-
ory of rodeo riders and our cowboy history. Another great museum that
recalls our Western heritage is the Buffalo Bill Cody Museum in Cody,
Wyoming. Dozens of museums, both small and large, in most western states tell parts of the story of what life was like when the West
was wild.

Dinosaur National Monument in Utah is a marvelous working
museum that gives a firsthand view of scientists at work uncovering the
prehistoric past. Visitors, many of whom are RVers, come away with a
far greater comprehension of the science of paleontology.

Due to my years as a member of the U.S. Navy in World War II, I love
to tour warships: the battleship *Alabama* at Mobile, the *Texas* at the San
Jacinto Battlefield Monument near Houston (a double-barreled attraction), the *Yorktown* at Charleston, the *Lexington* at Corpus Christi, and
the *Constitution* at Boston. Touring these ships, combined with reading all the literature displayed for tourists, helps one connect with our
great wars.

We've been to all of these places and have personally seen both the
attractions and the scores of RVs parked in the parking lots. It's obvious to me that we RVers are interested in seeing and knowing more
about our world and our history.

Also we have a leg up on those who travel by airplanes, cars, buses,
or trains because we visit in the comfort of our homes. Often our rig
is out in the parking lot of the attraction we are visiting, so we can
rest any time, eat any time, or even take a nap in between hitches of
touring. That makes for very easy, pleasant learning. Many fulltimers,
although lacking in extensive formal education, end up well educated
through practical observation and involvement.

New People, Places, and Things

Many people, especially those who are of retirement age, have led rather restricted lives. Until recent years, travel was much more limited than it is now. People often stayed close to home most of the time and normally took a vacation once a year, during which time they might have taken a long trip. Generally, their firsthand knowledge of other places was somewhat limited.

That can change drastically when you go fulltiming. You meet people with diverse backgrounds, you see places you've only read about, and you find yourself doing things you've never done before. Your circle expands; life becomes more interesting.

Excitement

I can't think of anything worse than going through life with nothing but dull routine day in and day out. To me, the idea of sitting in a rocking chair on a porch all day long and jawing with cronies or watching television for six or eight hours every evening is a boring way to live. I like to wake up with the prospect of going somewhere new or doing something exciting every day. I can't picture myself in a life without something to look forward to each day. Fulltimers have every opportunity to do that. All they have to do is select exciting places to visit and go there.

Security

Crime is rampant in America and, in some places, is getting worse. To add to all the "normal" crime (murders, robberies, rapes, assaults, thefts), we now have terrorism to cope with. Not since the frontier days have personal safety and protection of property been of such great concern. Just read the newspapers, watch television, or listen to the radio and you'll almost be convinced that we live in a war zone. In fact, many people in cities live behind locked, bolted doors and barred windows and never go out alone or at night. They must constantly be alert for purse-snatchers or muggers. They never know when they leave their homes if their belongings will be there when they return. Of course, nowadays, we have to add to our list of fears the threat of acts of terrorism.

When we lived in Los Angeles County (we left in the late 1970s), Margie always kept our doors locked, even in the daytime, since robberies and rapes during the day were not uncommon. And we lived in a supposedly quiet, safe, college community. Imagine what it is like to be a resident in one labeled "unsafe."

We've all seen investigative news programs showing how some older people in cities live in fear; some even suffer malnutrition because they are afraid to walk on streets in their own neighborhoods to go shopping.

The RV lifestyle is probably the most crime-free way to live. Quite simply, robbers, muggers, rapists, and murderers usually don't travel in trailers or motorhomes. Probably a major reason for the lack of crime in the lifestyle is due to the fact that RVers aren't dopers. Few crimes are committed in campgrounds or RV parks. Many RVers think nothing of leaving their rigs with doors open, walking at night alone in parks, or carrying their purses loosely. In most parks, there's a fence between the inhabitants inside and the general population outside. Some parks, especially those that cater to snowbirds, have guarded entry gates. It's always prudent to be careful, but in short, RVers live without having to fear their fellow man.

CHAPTER FIVE

My House: To Sell or Not to Sell?

Whether or not to sell the house can be the stickiest question that prospective fulltimers will face. The answer depends very much on the attitudes of the people involved (usually a couple). If they are convinced that they both want to sell, then the answer is obvious. If one or both have doubts that it is what they really want to do, however, then my advice is to hang on to it for a while. Undoubtedly, some people have strong emotional attachments to their houses, and, after selling them, get a bad case of seller's remorse, although I don't hear of many cases like that. I'm sure it would be a very difficult thing to live with—both for the person who is suffering and the one who has to put up with the sufferer.

It may be of some comfort to those who are having difficulty in deciding the issue of whether or not to sell the house to know that in over twenty years of presenting full-timing seminars to thousands of people, many of whom were fulltimers, that only one person ever told me that she would like to have her house back. In fact, I am always amused to see heads twist rather violently when I ask the question, "How many of you would like to have your house back?"

I think the mental process of deciding to sell one's house and the actual business that one has to go through in doing so is the problem time. After the deed is done, it's over and the problem goes away. After all, you aren't giving up your home, you are merely changing homes. You'll be surprised how quickly your RV feels like home.

Selling the House

Of course, if whether or not to go full time depends financially on the sale of the house, then the answer is obvious—you've got to sell. In many cases, the funds from the sale of the real estate are necessary for acquiring a full-time rig or for living expenses. In fact, the proceeds from the sale of a house are the primary source of income for many full-timers. In some cases, they sell for cash, invest the money, and receive regular interest or dividend payments. Others prefer to hold mortgages on their houses and receive the interest and principal payments over a long period of time. Although there is some risk involved, holding a mortgage can be an excellent way of receiving a fixed payment at an interest rate that can exceed bank interest rates. We found that to be the case when we opted for life on the road over twenty years ago. Although interest rates fluctuated over the many years that we held mortgages, in the long run, we were ahead of the game.

Keeping the House

RVers who go fulltiming or even extended-timing and leave houses behind are sometimes unknowingly setting themselves up for big problems in the future. Although it is possible to leave it in the hands of competent, responsible people, it is a situation fraught with potential problems. Just ask me. For twenty-three years, we've used our home in northern Idaho for about four months a year and traveled the rest.

We've experimented with various ways of handling the issue; some were winners, some weren't. Our experiences have ranged from "darn good" to "near disaster." Assaults by flood and fire were the highlights— to say nothing of the cost of keeping the place. We may not be there, but the bills are. Insurance, taxes, power, phone, and regular maintenance—these things are never-ending. But it's a penalty we're willing to pay to keep our very special home base in the Idaho panhandle. Like so many other extended-timers, we want to have our cake and eat it too! Based on our own experience, though, we conclude that it costs almost twice as much to live as an extended-time RVer if you keep a house.

Most years, we've left the house empty. Living in the country as we do, all our neighbors know when we are gone. They're great neighbors, all of whom keep an eye out for any untoward activity. One neighbor and good friend checks inside the house regularly. So, as long as we have honest neighbors, we're okay, but imagine the field day they could have if ever they decide to become burglars!

Even though we've tried to cover all bases in protecting our place, we've had some problems. The first winter away from home, we left our water pump on (we have our own water system). The neighbors who were checking the house called us in California where we were parked to report that, to their horror, they opened the door to a flooded house because a water pipe had frozen and burst. The water pump had run for several days, pouring water on the floor upstairs, then running down into the living room and on to the basement—an incredible mess. Water damage amounted to thousands of dollars, all of which was insured. The emotional damage was even greater and definitely not insured. But we survived and kept on RVing—with the water pump turned off now!

Although we did so with great trepidation, we tried renting the house once when we expected to be gone for two years. So we rented to a well-interviewed and referenced "perfect couple" who agreed to care for the place as if it were their own. Guess what? We came back to check on the place the next summer and found dead grass, dying trees, and a dirty house that we were lucky to have because our "perfect couple" had nearly burned it down. After repairing the charred deck and side of the house, we decided that our first experience as landlords would be our last.

Our experiences, coupled with those we have heard about from others, have led to these conclusions:

1. Renting out a house acquired specifically for that purpose may be a good way to create income, but renting out your *home* is not.

2. If you can find a responsible house sitter, great. However, be aware that what you see in that so-called responsible person may not be the reality.

3. Leaving a house vacant for long periods of time is risky—both from the standpoint of the danger of burglary or vandalism and the possibility of damage from broken pipes, wire, or gas lines.

4. Keeping a house while RVing extensively is both an emotional and financial drain on the owners. Unless there is an exceptionally strong reason not to do so, you are much better off if you sell it.

5. A final note: If you plan to leave your house empty, check with your insurance agent to be sure that you are complying with the company's occupancy clauses.

CHAPTER SIX

What Do I Do with My Possessions?

Most of us have a pack-rat instinct that makes us accumulate "things." Anyone who has lived in a house for many years, as most people who take up fulltiming have, has probably filled closets, drawers, shelves, attics, garages, and various other places with "stuff." We sometimes have fancier names for our things like *memorabilia, acquisitions, mementos*. I have another not-so-fancy name to add to that list: *crap*. It is unbelievable what we have in our accumulations of stuff, especially the stuff that has no practical use, doesn't fit, is out of date, is worn out, we don't look at, is broken, gives us no enjoyment, or otherwise is of no value. Men are particularly noted for keeping pants that don't fit them anymore and tools that are broken (men who wear size 40 pants still keep the 38s—some even the 36s—and none ever throws away a shovel with a broken handle—they're going to put in a new one some day) Our houses are loaded with stuff that won't even sell at a garage sale. Why do we keep it? It's the rat-pack instinct, something that we must divest ourselves of if we expect to go fulltiming. But how do you get rid of it? I have several suggestions garnered from years of interviewing fulltimers.

Packing Your Full-timing Rig

To pack properly, you need some rules. I believe these three will benefit you greatly if you follow them.

1. The "Year" Rule

This rule says that if you haven't used it in the past year, you probably
don't need it and shouldn't pack it. For example, clothes that you haven't
had on in the past year are prime candidates for leaving out. Either you
don't really care for them or they don't fit you. Take only your favorite
things, those that you have been putting on regularly in the past year.
Most fulltimers no longer need heavy winter clothing because they
expect to be in warm snowbird roosts when the snow flies up north.
However, I suggest taking some fairly heavy clothing because even in
the sunniest of climates, freezing temperatures occasionally hit. Most
fulltimers don't need a lot of fancy, dress clothing. Comfortable, casual
clothing is almost invariably right. But one dress outfit will prove useful on those rare occasions when one feels compelled to dress up.

The same rule applies to many other categories of "stuff": kitchen
utensils, for example, should be limited to a minimum of pots and pans,
skillets, some of the electric gadgets, etc. Special-use items like the
Thanksgiving turkey plate just might be expendable in a motorhome;
one set of dishes with service for four will be sufficient for most couples; and you don't need a set of sterling silver either.

2. The "Veto" Rule

Full-timing couples who, unfortunately, have different ideas about
whether some things are necessary or expendable usually pack together
for fulltiming. That's when you need the "veto" rule, which says that
each of the parties in the couple has the right to veto what the other is
trying to pack. For example, a woodworking hobbyist might try to

include a table saw with the "necessities," so his partner will have to say, "Veto." And when he sees her carrying an armload of photo albums of the kids and grandkids, it's his turn to say, "Veto." Of course, the partners must be compatible or the full-timing adventure will end before it ever starts.

3. The "Three-fourths" Rule

This rule says, Don't fill up all your compartments and drawers. Save some space because as sure as you are born, you'll accumulate more "crap" as you travel and you need spaces to put it.

The task of packing all the stuff you will need to live full time on the road is indeed a formidable one. When you consider that you will have to reduce the possessions you have in an average 2,000-square-foot, six-room house to what will fit in what is at best a 320-square-foot trailer or motorhome, you can see why you will have to be very selective in what you take with you and what you dispose. However, many RVs are designed with fulltimers in mind and, consequently, have a tremendous amount of storage capacity. The idea of a basement on an RV has revolutionized storage capability. And the way every nook and cranny inside is utilized for storage with cabinets, shelves, and drawers is amazing. The fact is that many large RVs—both towables and motorized—have storage capacities that will hold everything that the average fulltimer needs.

Getting Rid of the Rest

After you have intelligently packed your rig, you must do something with all the rest of your stuff. Of course, you can have a "moving sale" or auction and get rid of most of it, but that method will deprive your kids and grandkids of an opportunity to have some the things that will remind them of "home." So, I suggest that you first offer them an opportunity to choose items that they would like. In cases where there are several children, let them take turns in choosing items.

A nice feature in giving your stuff to kids is that it remains in the family. Special items like a china closet with a collection of pretty dishes or "Dad's chair" will still be where they can be seen on visits to your children.

When the kids and grandkids have done their thing, let other friends, relatives, and neighbors pick over what is left. End up by calling the Salvation Army or other charitable organization to pick up the items that are left (be sure to get a receipt for your generous donation!).

CHAPTER SEVEN

What Do I Do About Kids, Grandkids, and Relatives?

Some prospective fulltimers find giving up family too difficult, especially those who have routines where kids and grandkids come over every Sunday for the day. The huge meals that Grandma spends all day fixing and which vanish in a few minutes, crying babies, kids getting into forbidden things in the garage, blaring TVs and radios—all these normal family get-togethers that become established Sunday routines for some people are too ingrained for some people to surrender. The reality is that once you sell the house and hit the road, you can't have the family together every Sunday, and there will be extended periods when you won't see the grandchildren. Your contact with them will be primarily by letter, e-mail, or telephone. So if you are the kind who just has to have close physical contact with family, you won't be a very successful fulltimer.

Love Them but Leave Them

You don't have to quit loving your family to be a fulltimer, but you do have to leave them for extended periods of time. I'm sure that most fulltimers love their kids, grandkids, and other relatives as much as other families. Actually, in this day and age, many (most?) kids end up not only leaving home after high school, but move far away from their folks. In fact, one of the questions I often ask at seminars I am presenting is, "How many of you have kids who live in different states than you?" I'm not amazed any more at the tremendous showing of hands. It's just a fact that in our mobile society, kids grow up and do their thing. So, the point is that many retired couples considering fulltiming don't have to worry about leaving their kids and grandkids. They've already left.

One of the especially enjoyable aspects of fulltiming is being able to visit kids and other relatives at times of your own choosing. In cases where kids live considerable distances from each other, you have the option of going to them while remaining in your own home. You can pull up at an offspring's house, park in the driveway, and enjoy the kids and grandkids on your own terms. (Note: Here's a good time to *get even* with your children. Turn on *all* the lights in your RV, turn on the radio and TV—full blast, go open their refrigerator door, and just stand there for five minutes, or grab a carton of milk and drink directly from it; take a long, long shower and use all the hot water—*get even.*) With your RV hooked up to their services, you can enjoy your own bed, your own space when you want privacy, and your own things when you want them. And you are free to leave when the visit has worn down. All this transpires with very little disturbance of either household. It's a win-win for everyone.

Not all non-RVers understand the convenience of visiting others while remaining in their wheeled home. I can recall the first time we visited Margie's folks in a motorhome and they couldn't understand why we didn't want to occupy the spare bedroom they had prepared for us—to them, we were sleeping in the car. However, after a few days' trip with us in the motorhome, they understood why we felt the way we did.

My point is that living full time in an RV actually gives many parents and grandparents more opportunities to be with their loved ones than living in a conventional home. Not only that, the hassle involved in having or being houseguests is avoided. Everyone keeps his or her own space.

Although fulltiming may reduce the amount of time that families can be together, they often find that the *quality* of the time they spend with them compensates for the lack of *quantity*.

CHAPTER EIGHT

How Do I Keep in Touch?

Giving up a fixed place and taking to the road full time doesn't have to mean giving up contact with family and friends. Indeed, few of us are inclined to neglect regular communication with our grandkids, parents, and friends. Most of us on the road have developed patterns of communication that keep us within the swirl of family life even though we aren't there in person.

By Mail

Thanks to our efficient (generally) U.S. Postal Service, those who prefer the written word can keep in touch the old-fashioned way—letters. Although your post office will forward your mail for up to a year if you keep them informed of address changes, that doesn't work well if you are traveling considerably. The best way is to provide them with an address that you can keep as long as you are fulltiming.

One solution to the problem is to have your mail go to a son or daughter (or other close relative) who can weed out the junk mail and forward the rest to wherever you are or are going to be. Of course there will be the postage cost and a time lag in getting the mail. Plus, for those who move around a lot, there will be the need for phone calls to change addresses. However, it does give RVers a chance to talk to their offspring or relatives who are handling the mail.

A mail-forwarding service is the solution for most fulltimers. Not only is it quite reliable, it eliminates the chore for a family member. Most of the major clubs have mail-forwarding services—the Good Sam Club, Family Motor Coach Association, and the Escapees Club. Then there are private re-mail businesses, most of whom advertise in the classified sections of *Trailer Life, MotorHome, Highways,* and *Family Motor Coaching.* All of them have a very reasonable basic charge for handling the mail plus postage.

The program works this way: You are provided with an address with a "box number" at the club or service's headquarters. You provide everyone with whom you wish to correspond with that address and your mail goes there. You, in turn, notify the mail-forwarding service every week where you want your mail sent. That might be to a campground, friend, or relative that you expect to visit, or it can go to General Delivery. If you choose the latter, pick a small town that you intend to pass through in five to seven days. You choose the small town to avoid parking problems and waits in lines at large post offices. If, however, you are going to have your mail sent to General Delivery in a large city (which I strongly recommend against), make sure you have the correct zip code for the branch office where you prefer to pick up your mail.

By Telephone

Just a few years ago, cell phones and the service charges were so outrageously high that their regular use was a luxury only for those with deep pockets. However, that picture has changed enormously. Nowadays, most RVers have cell phones, many of which are quite inexpensive, and a variety of service plans, some of which even people of modest means can afford. The point is that no matter where RVers are—in a park or on the road—their families and friends are just as close by phone as they when they lived in houses. Moms and Dads can keep up with the daily lives of their kids and grandkids and vice versa. Margie often chats with ours as we travel down the highways.

Not only is cell phone service a boon to families and friends keeping in touch, it is a wonderful service to have when emergencies arise—both health and mechanical. It's so convenient to call for that emergency service directly from where the emergency is happening.

E-mail

The electronics age has brought with it a form of communication that RVers are finding ideal—e-mail. Combining leisurely letter writing and instantaneous transmission, this medium allows a full-timing co-pilot to compose lengthy epistles as they travel, as well as when they are parked at night. Then with a simple phone connection, whammo, the letter is immediately in the kids' computers. In fact, the same letter can go to any number of people if you wish. Many campgrounds have Internet connections at spaces, and inventions and improvements in electronics will enable us to do all kinds of new, improved wireless communications. Every year brings new electronic toys, some of them of special interest to RVers.

For example, I have no doubt that, like the cell phone and computers, as the price goes down, photo- and videophones will be common with fulltimers in the years to come. While co-piloting, Grandma can talk to and see her grandkids as Grandpa tools down the highway.

So, as you can see, there's no need for fulltimers to pull the communications plug on their families and friends just because they have unplugged their connections to a particular piece of real estate.

CHAPTER NINE

How Do I Handle Financial Affairs While on the Road?

I have no doubt that in the future banking in the conventional way will be almost entirely superseded by electronic means. It's here now, but there's still a generation that likes to see the paper—the checks—both outgoing and incoming. Younger generations who have been brought up with computers will quickly adapt to paperless banking, which will be a lot easier for fulltimers. But until that time, many fulltimers will need solutions for doing conventional banking while living an unconventional lifestyle. Actually it's not that difficult.

Banking by Mail

Deposits can be made by mail. Banks provide deposit envelopes and deposit slips for that purpose. We've been mailing checks to our bank for over twenty years and have never had a one get lost. To make depositing even easier, you can arrange to have all regular checks, especially those from governments or company pensions, *direct deposited*. Then you don't have to go through the receiving, endorsing, and mailing procedures.

Handling on-the-Road Expenses

Since most people paid their bills by mail even before they took to the road, there's really no change when they go fulltiming. Even though that method works well, I suggest that all prospective fulltimers explore the possibility of using electronic bill paying.

Paying regular travel and living expenses on the road is best done by credit card. Most businesses take plastic, so there's no point in carrying a lot of cash. Not only can you use your credit cards to pay for things, many of them double as ATM cards, which can keep you supplied with necessary cash.

We use credit cards for nearly all of our purchases—even in grocery stores where they are accepted. Not only is it convenient, many card companies offer prizes or rebates on your total purchases at the end of the year. But we always pay our credit card bill before interest is charged—something that one has to watch because the time between billing and receiving the money is growing shorter with some banks. Since fulltimers often have a considerable lag-time in getting their mail, this could prove to be a problem. However, it is one that could be eliminated with a bill-paying arrangement with your bank.

The only downside to using credit cards is that many service stations charge more for card purchases than they do for cash. If you have a large fuel tank, sometimes it pays to use the ATM machine and pay the charge imposed there so you can pay cash for a big load of fuel. Some campgrounds won't give both a discount for club membership and take a credit card.

There are many kinds of cards issued by various agencies including debit cards, which are in effect universal, instant checks. It's another way to eliminate paper banking.

I suggest that all full-timing couples get two credit cards, that is, two different kinds of cards. Get two of each, but each person carries a different card and the extras are put in the fireproof box that everyone should carry for important papers. By carrying different cards, if one person loses their wallet or purse, you can cancel that card and get the other card out of the fireproof box. That way, both persons are always in the credit business even if a card has to be cancelled.

Handling Tax Payments on the Road

In March, I often hear RVers say that they have to go home (or where home used to be) to do their income taxes. That's totally unnecessary for most people. Unless you are in a business with extensive records, you can do it all by mail. Our taxes aren't exactly overcomplicated, but neither are they simple, and we haven't been home for taxes in over twenty-five years. We simply keep our records with us and add receipts and other documentation as we go along. A wonderful help is that banks, investment firms, and other financial institutions provide all pertinent tax information in concise form at the end of the year. Then at tax time, I sort everything out, do all the preliminary figuring, and mail the information to our accountant. He puts it all on the proper forms and sends it to us for signatures (and sometimes more money) and to mail to the IRS and the State of Idaho. I'm sure that some people need to discuss their financial affairs at great length with their accountants, but, in most cases, it is just taking up the accountant's time (which, believe me, he is charging for).

Nowadays, many people do their tax reporting by computer. The IRS expects an ever-growing use of this method.

In short, there is seldom any need for a person to be present to handle normal financial matters. It can all be done by mail, telephone, fax, or e-mail.

CHAPTER TEN

What Health Care Preparations Do I Need to Make?

W e often refer to the elderly as being in their senior years, the mature years, or other such euphemisms. Most sociologists don't use fancy terms; they simply called it "old age." But, whatever you call it, it's a time when human bodies are more prone to get out of whack, or for those that are already malfunctioning to get worse. Therefore, since retirement usually occurs in the early to mid-60's, it's also the period that might be labeled the Breaking-Down Years. It's a time when the term *health care* takes on additional significance. It may become a major concern for those who are considering being away from normal health-care facilities and, especially, their own doctors.

Since the variety and severity of health problems is almost infinite, it is difficult to generalize about how to approach the question of health care on the road. However, there are some basic preparations most of us can make that will enable us to cope better with our ills, both present and future.

Preparing for Health Care on the Road

Probably the most important element in health care is to know what your problems are, if any, and to give them proper treatment—hence the need for regular and thorough physical examinations. *Regular* has different meanings in different situations and with different doctors. Some physicians advocate annual checkups. Others suggest more frequent exams and still others recommend complete physicals only every other year. Whatever the term, the point is to keep aware of your condition so oncoming ailments can be identified and treated early and preparations for further treatment can be planned for.

Not only should you have accurate knowledge of your physical condition, you should have medical records with you as you travel. Any doctor nowadays will make copies of your record and give them to you. With these in hand, you are in a position to save both time and money when you stop for treatment or assistance at a doctor's office, clinic, or hospital on your travels. Incidentally, these records should be kept in your fireproof box along with your other important papers.

If you take pills or other medications, you should always keep a good supply on hand. One of the wonders of the electronic age is that prescriptions put on computers at drug chains (Wal-Mart, Walgreen's, etc.) make your medicines available anywhere there is a store of that kind. Of course, if you buy your pills from mail-order houses, they can be sent to wherever you tell them. Another source of medicines if you are on the Mexican border (Arizona, Texas, and California) is in drugstores in the Mexican towns that are just across the border from popular snowbird "roosts."

Walk-in Clinics

One of the big changes in the availability of medical services has been the advent of "walk-in" clinics. Like the fast-food industry, you can almost get drive-through treatment for less-serious health problems. Most cities and large towns have them. We've sought services at them several times over the years and have generally been pleased at the quality of treatment we have received.

Know First Aid

Every fulltimer should have some basic knowledge of first aid and a reasonably complete first-aid kit. We also carry a blood-pressure monitor that requires no special skill to operate. Knowledge of CPR can be a lifesaver. Some rally programs include free CPR lessons, and they are offered by many city agencies, such as fire departments and organizations like the Red Cross.

Handling Major Health Emergencies

Looking at the grim side for a moment, let's ask what you do in extreme health emergencies while on the road. Let's assume it becomes necessary to have major surgery with a fairly long period of recuperation and frequent attention from a doctor. The good news is that most RVers are within a few hours (often only minutes) of complete medical facilities. For those who wander way off the beaten path, cell phones and helicopters generally keep people well connected to medical lifelines.

Although one might be far away from one's former (or present) home, there are some good aspects to having surgery done in a strange city if you are an RVer. In fact, it can be the easiest and best situation you could ask for under what is an unfortunate circumstance. Most hospitals will permit you to park your RV in their parking lot where the well spouse can live while the sick or injured spouse recuperates. It eliminates the problem of being stuck in a waiting room day and night or running back and forth to hotels. Actually the well spouse can perform the normal functions of living while being very near his or her loved one.

If there is a long period of recuperation, the RV can be the perfect place. Not long ago, a friend of ours had quadruple bypass surgery in a city far from his home. Rather than have his wife drive home, they spent the period of recuperation in a nearby campground just a few blocks from the hospital. His doctor was close by, and according to my friend, he was "spared the disruptions of well-wishers and their grim stories of people who had awful aftereffects from bypass surgery."

Although my beliefs and comments about how fortunate RVers are to be living that way when emergency surgeries occur date back many years, my ideas were proved to us several years ago when I collapsed in a strange city and required five bypasses. I was in the hospital for eight days while Margie lived in the motorhome nearby.

On an even grimmer note, death is always a possibility while on the road. Not only should the normal preparations be made for the disposition of your estate, but of your remains. I have witnessed the utter confusion that reigned when a woman died one night in a park where the couple had stopped for the night. The husband was totally distraught, and the park manager was faced with a very difficult problem. That problem can be avoided by another level of planning.

Margie and I have planned for our inevitable demise by arranging for some of the details connected with that event. We carry cards that give the toll-free number of a funeral parlor where we have already paid for the disposition of our remains. Our children will be notified as well as all concerned agencies (Social Security, Veteran's Administration, etc.). And, finally, we have chosen a plot in the family cemetery where our tombstone is already in place. We don't consider this a morbid preparation. Rather, we consider it a commonsense solution to what could be a very difficult problem. Our children know of our plan and know that it is done out of love and concern for them.

Maintaining a Regular Health Program

My last, but certainly not the least, important recommendation for maintaining the best health is proper eating and exercise. It is my observation that, as a group, RVers enjoy better health than folks of similar ages in the general population. The reason must be that they exercise more—walking, bicycling, dancing, and swimming. Many snowbird parks offer aerobics, dancing, and other forms of exercise classes. All fulltimers should have a regular exercise regimen, be careful of what and how much they eat, and pay attention to their weight. It's so easy to get into bad health habits when you're "just loafin'." It may not be easier but it's a lot better to be fit.

We find that a morning walk, regardless of where we are, goes part of the way toward keeping reasonably fit. Actually, our little dog, Suzie, demands that walk, so she's doing us a favor. And when traveling, walks in new areas can be especially interesting. I like to look at the other RVs in campgrounds and sometimes stop to chat with their owners.

We hear regularly of new studies that show that being active both physically and mentally is important for good health. In fact, several studies show that people who continue to work do better than those who don't. Perhaps the best recipe for good health as one travels is to combine it with some kind of mental or physical labor part of the time.

What Are the Dos and Don'ts About Insurance?

You can be fully insured in all respects as a fulltimer, but some companies either do not insure people who don't live in permanent houses or their coverages are inadequate. Consequently, your on-the-road insurance shopping may include more than comparisons of rates and services. Up front, you must include the question, Do you insure fulltime RVers?

Vehicle Insurance

As a fulltimer, your RV will in all probability be your most valuable possession, so it is extremely important that it be well covered by insurance. This is where your question, Do you insure fulltime RVers? is important because many companies don't.

However, there are plenty of companies that do. Among them are some of the major companies—RV Alliance America, RV Advantage, and Foremost. Both the Good Sam Club and Family Motor Coach Association offer insurance plans that cover fulltimers.

Whatever insurance company you choose should offer a *replacement value* or *agreed value* option. Although it costs a little more, you should take it; otherwise you might find, as we did, that a total loss of your rig could be quite costly. We had a two-month-old, 40-foot motorhome completely burn up. Although we were insured, there was a thousand-dollar deductible and twenty-five-cents-per-mile deduction. Plus we lost the sales tax and license that we had paid. We had what was essentially a new motorhome, but we didn't get enough out of it to get a new one. With *replacement* value, you get a new rig or the *agreed* value, which is usually high enough to get a new rig including tax and license.

Emergency Road Service

A special kind of insurance that every RVer needs is emergency road service. Having a breakdown in a car is bad enough, but having a breakdown in a large RV can be devastating. Even changing a tire on a motorhome is beyond the capability of most motorhomers, especially on diesel rigs, and having to be towed a hundred miles can devastate a budget.

Some auto clubs and insurance policies cover emergency road service. For example, my motorhome insurance includes emergency road service and my auto insurance does the same with some limitations. Many RV clubs, associations, and companies offer that service—Good Sam Club, FMCA, Escapees, KOA, Camping World, Coast to Coast, etc. Although most of them offer the same basic service, each has special features and there is some variation in costs. I suggest that you compare several of them and choose the one that you feel most comfortable with. Incidentally, we had the Good Sam Club's service when our motorhome burned up. One call from us was all it took, and the burned-out hulk and debris were all cleaned up promptly and thoroughly without hassle.

Health Insurance

Although many fulltimers are at an age when they have Medicare, it covers only a portion of a medical bill. The rest usually comes from a supplemental insurance. AARP has plans that are good anywhere, but some HMOs limit service to their own facilities. So, members of HMOs need to find out if they will be covered while on the road.

I'm often asked by younger full-timer wannabes how they can be insured when they aren't old enough for Medicare and don't have jobs with insurance coverage. That's a tough one to answer. Private plans are available but they're very expensive. And at this writing, there's no insurance company with a special, reasonably priced full-timer's plan that is open to all ages.

Life Insurance

Life insurance policies aren't affected by moving from one place to another or to a life on the road, but it is important that you keep your agent informed of your address. And, regardless of who your insurers and what coverage they provide, it is important that you take your policies with you and keep them in your fireproof box.

What Papers Should I Pack?

A fact of life (and death) in this age is that we live and die fully documented. Most of the aspects of daily living are in some way connected with written records. Indeed, such documents play so important a role in our lives that if we should suddenly lose them all, I'm not sure we could function very long.

We vary individually in our paper needs. Some are basic for everyone, but others are essential for select individuals. Let's take a look at some of the various categories of common documents that you should have with you.

Vehicle Titles and Registrations

Obviously, every RVer has vehicle title and registration documents, and they should be with us in our rigs. State laws always require registrations. The need for a title may occur only infrequently; however, there's always the possibility of running into a deal on a new RV that is irresistible, or one of those horrible occasions when your machine gives up its ghost and you are forced to get something new. Of course you also need those documents for your tow vehicle or your towed car.

Birth Certificates and Passports

You never know when you're going to have to provide verification of citizenship.

When going to Mexico or Canada, it may or may not be needed, but it's nice to have the proof—just in case. However, if you decide to travel to a foreign country, you will probably need a passport. It isn't something that you get overnight, so it should be taken care of before you start fulltiming if there's any chance at all that you will go out of the country.

Financial Records

Most financial records can be stored in your computer; however, some records need to be with you in "hard copy." You can store records pertaining to bank accounts, mortgages, notes, stocks and bonds, and other financial affairs on a disc, but in some instances, you need the actual document. Sort all financial records out carefully before you hit the road and determine what you need to have with you.

Wills

Everyone should have a will no matter how modest his or her estate, and a copy of that will should be among the papers you take with you. You never know when you might want to look at it and make changes.

Military Veterans

Vets should take a copy of their discharge papers with them. One reason is that in order to obtain the limited medical benefits that all honorably discharged veterans are entitled to, they must have a copy of your discharge to their application.

Fireproof Box

All valuable papers—insurance, wills, discharge papers, financial and medical records—should be kept in a fireproof safe or box in your RV. We had one when our motorhome burned, and its contents were the only thing saved from the fire. For less than fifty dollars for a Sentry fireproof box (Wal-Mart, Lowe's, Staples, etc.), you can have the comfort of knowing your valuable papers will be safe in a fire that completely destroys your rig.

CHAPTER THIRTEEN

Should I Take My Pet?

I understand well the feelings of those who wish to take their pets with them in their RVs. We love animals and always had dogs and cats when we lived a "regular" life, but we decided at the beginning of our extended RVing not to take them with us. We know that taking care of them properly requires adjustments in one's travel mode that we weren't willing to make. So for nearly twenty years, we traveled without pets.

That changed, however, almost four years ago when a little stray dog refused to stay away from our motorhome while we were parked at my sister's house in California. It was the grungiest little animal I had every seen—long, filthy fur, tail down, and bedraggled looking. I chased it away several times during a two-day period but on the third morning when I found it curled up on one of my sister's patio chairs, I couldn't stand it any longer. I took her to a dog groomer, had her all shorn and cleaned up. She came out a cute little thing. Next, off to a veterinarian where she received attention for an infection. After that, to a pet store for collar, leash, and dog food. And I had a dog that I named Suzie.

We changed some of our travel procedures and made adjustments in many of our routines to accommodate Suzie's wants. And now we wonder how we ever got along without her. She's such a delight to travel with— such good company—never grumpy, always curious. The fact that she loves rest areas makes me pull in much more frequently than I ordinarily would. That's a good thing because when crossing the country, which we do a couple of times a year, I sometimes stay at the wheel longer than

I should. Now I stop at least every two hours for a walk with Suzie. Of course we start every day and end it with nice, long walks in campgrounds.

Some Considerations for Pet Owners

If you have an animal, be it dog, cat, bird, or whatever, there are few reasons why you shouldn't take your pet with you in your travels. True, a few campgrounds and RV parks don't permit them at all, but generally they are allowed—with reasonable restrictions. Few public campgrounds exclude pets; however, Florida state parks do (a rule that is under pressure to revise).

However, the big questions are those that only you can answer: Are you willing to give the pet the attention it requires? Are you willing to give proper consideration to your fellow campers and the rules and regulations in parks? You have to face the fact that having an animal restricts your activities. For instance, you arrive at a city like Boston, and you want to tour all the historical places. In the first place, as in most large cities, you will be camped a long way from downtown. If you tour in your car, you can take your pet, but, usually, you will have to leave it in the car while you sightsee, thereby limiting the time away from your car. Or you can take a tour bus—but your dog can't. So what happens when you are on an eight-hour tour? Of course you have to leave it in your RV while you are gone. Chances are—if it is a dog—it will bark, perhaps continuously while you are gone. And you might hear from your neighbors or the park manager when you return. Certainly, that sort of treatment isn't fair to the dog or to other RVers.

Consider Your Neighbors

Without intending to raise a controversy, I'd like to emphasize that inconsiderate pet owners create some of the major problems for campground owners. They're the ones who disobey campground and commonsense rules, the ones who believe that their dogs are exempt from the leash rules, that Fifi's doo-doo is okay anywhere she decides to deposit it, and that there's no need to pick it up. They're also the ones who feel that it's all right for their dogs to "express themselves" by barking whenever they feel like it, or who believe that their pet's behavior is always perfectly accepted by others. Believe me, it isn't. I'm amazed at how many apparently kind, intelligent, and generally considerate people are completely irrational in their attitudes about acceptable pet behavior.

A few years ago, I had the misfortune to encounter the most ridiculous pair of pet owners I ever met. They parked beside me in a campground that had clearly stated pet rules, which, of course, included a leash rule. Despite the rules, they allowed their Doberman to roam as he pleased outside their coach. On the second day, as I got out of *my car in my space,* as I put my left leg out of the door, the dog rushed up and grabbed me. Fortunately, I had on heavy jeans and the bite didn't break the skin, but it did hurt. I yelled. The dog's owner was outside his coach, and he asked what the matter was. When I told him, "Your dog bit me," his reply was, "But my dog doesn't bite." Those words were repeated as the lady appeared at the door. Unbelievable! Neither could comprehend the reality. Obviously to them, I was making something up. They're the kind of people who make life difficult for all dog owners.

I could have made life difficult for those people with a lawsuit, but I didn't. However, I reported the incident to the campground owner, who immediately evicted them—still protesting that their dog doesn't bite!

In short, there's little reason for you not to take your pet if you want to; but if you do, there's every reason for you to take care of it and your fellow campers properly.

CHAPTER FOURTEEN

Should I Take a Weapon?

Without the backing of an objective study, I think I would be safe in saying that well over half of all RVs on the road have some kind of weapon in them. In most cases, that weapon is a gun—generally a handgun. It is a fact of American life that most people have a gun or guns in their houses and houses on wheels are no exception. The only difference is that in most states, having a handgun in your RV is a violation of their laws.

Legal or Not?

While it is not my intent to get embroiled in the "right to keep and bear arms" controversy, I think we should all be aware of the fact that having a firearm in one's possession can get a person into trouble with the law. The federal government, all states, some counties, and many municipalities have gun laws. I read a study recently that stated that there are over 21,000 gun laws in the United States. Unfortunately, those laws aren't uniform and what may be legal in one place might not be legal in another.

Although we may claim that our homes on wheels are just as much of "castles" as our regular homes on the ground and that we are entitled to have firearms in our homes, not all law-enforcement officers, judges, and juries agree. In fact, I was once contacted by a lady who ended up with a felony conviction and a stiff sentence for having a concealed weapon (a loaded revolver under her bed) in a motor vehicle. The judge and jury did not agree that her motorhome was a home in the accepted sense. They considered it a vehicle first (the written law in many states), that she had violated a state law, and she was found guilty. A state appellate court upheld her conviction.

Whether you and I or anyone else agree or disagree with the court's decision is irrelevant. The only thing that counts is what the laws say and how judges and juries interpret them. It behooves us to know something about those laws if we are going to take guns with us in our RVs. An excellent synopsis of each state's laws can be found in *Traveler's Guide to the Firearm Laws of the Fifty States*, a state-by-state brief summary of gun laws (available at www.lifeonwheels.com).

Most of the laws that might get RVers in trouble are those that apply to "concealed weapons," which means handguns. To give you some idea of how varied those laws are, in most states, a gun in a glove compartment is illegal, yet in a few others, it is perfectly lawful. Most states have laws against having a weapon within reach of the driver, but in at least one state, it is permissible to have a loaded handgun on your seat with you as long as it is in "plain view." Indeed, the laws pertaining to handguns are many and complicated. The RVer who chooses to take one in his "vehicle" should be aware of the risk of being charged with a law violation if a law enforcement officer discovers it.

However, there is an alternative to carrying an illegal weapon in your RV but still permit you to have a gun. Take a rifle or shotgun—particularly the latter and, especially, a pump shotgun. Stop to think about it: You are a burglar prowling around someone's trailer or motorhome when all at once you hear the clack-clack of a shell being chambered into a pump shotgun. Every man (and most women) knows that sound. It would be especially scary knowing that it is going to be used on you. What will you do? Run, of course—what any sensible person would do under the circumstances. Besides, if you're actually going to shoot at someone in the dark (a dumb thing to do), aren't your chances of hitting them a heck of a lot better with a shotgun than a pistol?

Firearms in Other Countries

RVers traveling to Canada or Mexico would be wise to investigate carefully the laws of those countries before attempting to take any kind of firearm into them. They are very different from ours.

Canada does not permit handguns at all. With certain reservations, they do normally permit RVers to take rifles or shotguns into their country. First, you must be sure to declare the gun at the border when asked if you have any firearms. Failure to do so and a subsequent search of your rig revealing the gun's presence is a guarantee of a problem. Secondly, if asked why you are taking the gun, your response must satisfy the inspector, e.g., going hunting, attending a skeet shoot, but definitely not for self-protection.

If you should be charged with a violation of Canada's gun laws, you will be familiar with the legal process that follows because our legal systems are basically the same.

Mexico is another matter. Very simply, Mexico says, "No guns." If one is discovered in your rig, you will probably be in more trouble than you've ever been in your life. And the really bad news is that you will not be entitled to the legal processes that we are familiar with in this country. It could be a very costly experience in money, or, worse yet, it could be serious jail time. If you are afraid to travel in Mexico without a firearm, you should not go there.

Know How to Use Your Weapon

If you are going to carry a weapon, presumably for protection, know how to use it. Too many people have had their own guns used on them because they didn't know how to use it in the way they planned.

And, finally, bear in mind that if you actually shoot someone, you will probably end up with a long, perhaps expensive, tangle with the law. Even if there is no legal complication, you might suffer emotionally forever.

CHAPTER FIFTEEN

Should I Join a Membership Campground?

A wonderful aspect of fulltiming is that one's options on how to go about it are numerous and varied. However, that makes tough decisions necessary at times, decisions which may directly affect your pocketbook.

A question that I am frequently asked is, "What do you think about campground memberships?" My answer is always, "They're great for some people and worthless for others. You have everything in between."

I have questioned membership owners all over the country and have asked many attendees at my seminars what they think. When I ask, "How many of you own memberships?" I have a show of hands. Then when I ask, "If you could do it all over again, how many of you would buy that membership?" some hands go down. Many fulltimers find memberships a great solution to the problem of having places to stay. In fact, some of them own more than one membership and seldom use independent parks. Of course, they plan their travels so that they will always be near a membership park at night. They feel that their memberships were a good buy and a money saver.

On the other hand, there are those who buy memberships without thoroughly considering how those park plans will fit in with their travel plans. After they have made their purchases, they find that where they want to travel doesn't coincide with membership park locations and they end up not getting the benefits they thought they would get. Of course, some of those disappointed buyers succumbed to a sales pitch that painted a picture that didn't work in their cases.

Travel First–Join Later

I would suggest that if you are a beginning fulltimer you should get some experience on the road before investing in any membership, especially if you are the type who has a very indefinite travel schedule. After a few months on the road, you might decide that structured travel, that is, having to stay in specific places and conform to specific reservation rules, is not to your taste. On the other hand, you might decide that the plus side, particularly the security provided by reservations and quality of facilities, far outweighs any inconvenience caused by rules and regulations.

Consider the Cost

Most experienced fulltimers take a hard look at the economics of memberships. With prices often in the $4,000-plus price range, and annual fees, it should be obvious that from a financial standpoint, it takes a lot of nights of camping to reach the break-even point. One must also consider that the cash invested draws no interest as it would if it were in a savings account. And a financed membership costs interest. Tally up the whole cost of a financed membership and you might find that for your purposes, you are paying more than you really expected to pay for overnight accommodations.

But saving money is only one of the objectives of owning a campground membership. Sometimes the features offered by a particular program fit right into one's notions of RVing. Some people like going to the same places regularly, where they have friends and activities they especially like. People who buy memberships to get these features are buying *fun*—and there's no way to put a price tag on that.

A factor that you should investigate before plunking down thousands of dollars is the financial strength of the company selling memberships. A hard fact is that several memberships companies have had serious financial problems and some have gone bankrupt.

If you know you would like to belong to a particular organization, take a look at "used" memberships. There are lots of them available. Look in the classified section of RV publications or find a membership resale booth at an RV show. You'll find that you can find them at greatly discounted prices.

Regardless of where you buy a membership, be sure that you understand all the financial obligations that you incur when you sign a contract. Many have on-going fees that are difficult to cancel if you ever want out.

So, to repeat my advice at the beginning of this chapter, campground memberships are a product that might be just the ticket for you. It might solve many of the issues that face full-time RVers in terms of finances, good accommodations, and emotional needs. On the other hand, you might spend your money on an expensive product that you find not suited to your needs. You are the buyer so *caveat emptor*.

My suggestion is simply that you consider carefully what you are getting before you give up your hard-earned bucks. And beware of high-pressure salesmen. If a salesman is putting the pressure on you to buy a "fabulous offer *good only today*," give serious thinking about what is so special today that makes the same price no good tomorrow. Sleep on it. Then make a decision the next morning.

CHAPTER SIXTEEN

Should I Join an RV Club?

Many fulltimers find that membership in an RV club—or several clubs—is an asset to their lifestyle. While most of the time they're on their own, club members usually make it a point to attend rallies several time a year where they can visit with old friends and make new ones. It isn't uncommon for club members to meet up along the road or even travel together for periods of time. Clubs provide the opportunity for people to get together for socializing and learning.

Choosing a Club

There are dozens of RV clubs. Some have affiliations with businesses and some are independent. Many RV manufacturers sponsor "name-brand" clubs, some of which are company owned and managed, while others are independent. Some clubs are huge while others are quite small.

The largest group of all is the Good Sam Club, which has over one million members. Because of its enormous size, it is divided into local chapters, which in turn belong to state groups, then into regions, and finally the national organization. Rallies are held at all levels, but the primary group is the local chapter, which may meet at regular intervals (monthly, bi-monthly). State rallies are held once a year. A national rally is also held once a year. Most club members who are not fulltimers participate at the local level rallies, which are held a relatively short distances from members' homes. However, fulltimers often make it a point to attend the huge annual national rallies.

For motorhomes, there is the Family Motor Coach Association, which has a membership of over 100,000—and growing fast. Unlike the Good Sam Club, which is open to members with any type of RV, FMCA is geared to motorhome owners only.

Both the Good Sam Club and FMCA publish monthly magazines that are chock-full of information about the RV lifestyle—places to go, how to handle problems, and new products. Smaller clubs usually publish newsletters that are generally restricted to club news.

A club that I recommend to all fulltimers is the Escapees, developed specifically as a network of people on the road full time. Its activities are related primarily to RVers (any RV type) who want the information and security that the club offers. Much emphasis is placed in making fulltiming affordable to people of modest means.

One of the unique aspects of Escapees is that it owns over a dozen campgrounds in which it rents spaces to members at very inexpensive rates. Spaces in some of the parks are leased long term and, in others, spaces may be purchased.

A pioneering effort by the Escapees to care for the health needs of fulltimers who have become ill or partially incapacitated is the development of a facility they call CARE. That facility permits RVers who have health problems but are still able to live in their RV to park across the road and get to and from the CARE building to receive attention to their health needs, including nutrition. The club has many rallies where it offers RV products and seminars related to RVing.

Escapees greet each other with hugs instead of handshakes, which says a lot about the organization.

Reasons for Joining a Club

Different personalities, attitudes, and interests make it impossible for a single club to serve all fulltimers, but there are a few basic factors that induce most people to join.

Fellowship

Clubs bring people together, people with at least two basic interests—RVing and other people. Interests may vary, but when they're together at rallies, club members are birds of a feather and the rally is one big party.

Many clubs serve special personal situations. For example, there are several clubs for RVers who travel solo. Some are single because of the death of a spouse, some are divorced, and some are simply single. Many churches have camping clubs. Obviously, their common interest includes their religious preference. Whatever the reason, they enjoy the benefits of being with people with similar circumstances.

Caravans and Tours

Many clubs, including all the big ones, offer caravans or tours for their members. Trips to Alaska, Canada, Mexico, Europe, Africa, and Australia/New Zealand, as well as many tours within the United States, are led by wagonmasters who handle all the details—route, campground reservations, many of the dinners, side trips, and activities.

It's an easy way to travel, especially to foreign countries where you don't speak the language and don't know the customs.

Discounts and Special Benefits

Most of the large clubs have arranged for members to receive discounts at various facilities and on RV accessories and services. In fact, most memberships refund their cost in savings at campgrounds alone.

CHAPTER SEVENTEEN

How Do I Choose a Snowbird Roost?

RVers might have different views on the best way to RV, but there is one point on which they all agree: When it gets cold up north, go south! Disagreements are only about where to roost in the sunny south.

Following the Sun

The Sun Belt stretches from the Atlantic to the Pacific and includes nine to thirteen states, depending on who's calling the shots. Of these, four states probably get ninety percent of the snowbird business: Florida, Texas, Arizona, and California. When an RV snowbird says he's going south, the odds are that he will be going to one of these states.

To further narrow the bounds of "snowbird roosts," those who go to Florida will probably land in the central part of the state or on the Gulf Coast. Those who winter in Texas generally go to the Lower Rio Grande Valley, a less-than-100-mile stretch of land reaching from McAllen to South Padre Island. The Phoenix area, generally, and Mesa, specifically, are the most popular spots for Arizona birds. However, there is a large contingent in Yuma and growing flocks in Tucson and Casa Grande. Southern California birds generally settle in Riverside, Imperial, and San Diego counties, which include the original snowbird haven, Hemet, and now encompasses the fast-growing area that stretches from Indio to Palm Springs. So, despite the fact that the Sun Belt is indeed a large geographical area, RV snowbirds follow the old saying that "birds of a feather flock together"—and end up in big bunches in relatively few places.

Choosing Your Place in the Sun

We have tried all the popular snowbird roosts, most several times, and we like certain features about each. However, each has some aspects that we don't care for. It isn't a clear-cut case where one roost is far superior to all others. It comes down to a matter of personal preference based on a variety of reasons.

Since we prefer a dry climate to one that is humid, our favorite region is the Southwest. Consequently, after over twenty years of exploring all areas thoroughly, we have settled on Arizona, more specifically, Yuma. We like the small-town atmosphere, generally modest park prices, adequate shopping facilities, and absolutely super desert climate. As a matter of fact, I'm writing this right now in mid-February and every day this week has been sunny and in the mid- to high 70s. Plus, we have several good friends here, and it's close to Southern California where we have many relatives.

Although we prefer Yuma, I don't recommend it for everyone. For someone who likes big-city services, they would be much better off to opt for Mesa or Tucson. If you're into lofty cultural events, you should be aware that in Yuma the ballet is called "clogging." And the opera would more likely star a country singer. On the other hand, there's neither real traffic congestion nor smog.

Snowbirds have a tendency to go directly south, that is, Easterners tend to go to Florida, Midwesterners to Texas and Florida, and Westerners to Arizona and California. In spite of the fact that they often have all the time in the world, they usually opt for places nearest to their former homes. That's unfortunate for them, in a way, because I suspect that some would prefer other areas if they were only willing to travel a couple of days longer.

Common Aspects of Snowbird Roosts

Basically, most areas popular with snowbirds have a number of characteristics in common. The most important, of course, is generally warm weather. I say generally because all areas get unusually cold or otherwise disagreeable weather at times. We have been in Orlando in January and heard on the news that it snowed in Phoenix; conversely, this winter, while in Yuma, we heard of a terrible freeze in Tampa. Once we were in the Rio Grande Valley after a freeze the winter before that left palm trees with dead tops—frozen. The point is, if you judge an area on the weather extremes—hot, cold, or windy—all of them have some bad times. But, generally, all of them are what snowbirds seek—sunshine.

Although a warm climate is the primary objective, there are other factors that make places popular with snowbirds. Good parks are a must, with a variety that ranges from simple, low-priced ones to expensive resort types with amenities like clubhouses, swimming pools, hot tubs, game and craft rooms, ballrooms, even golf courses. And there must be lots of restaurants, golf courses, malls, and good health care facilities. Individual preferences may make certain natural features more important, for example, good fishing or, for boondockers, their special spot in a Southwestern desert.

I recommend that before settling on a roost, that wannabe snowbirds spend their first winter trying out all the major snowbird areas before concluding they've found the right one. I suggest starting at either California or Florida and working your way across the country, spending several weeks in each region at several different towns and parks.

Get a feel for the area. Don't expect in a short, few-days' visit to get a completely accurate picture of an area. It takes some "soaking up." A person who has the misfortune to stop at any snowbird area when the wind is blowing, the mercury is down, the rain is torrential, or the bugs are fierce, may totally misjudge the long-term advantages of that area. Bear in mind that all snowbird areas have the best winter weather in the nation, but all also have their bad moments.

And, by all means, bear this in mind: When you are knee-deep in snow, bundled up in your heaviest coat, face red from the biting wind in Boston or Chicago or Omaha or Cheyenne, even the *worst* weather in Tampa or Harlingen or Mesa or Hemet is better than what you have.

CHAPTER EIGHTEEN

How Much Does Fulltiming Cost?

Probably the question most asked by prospective fulltimers is, How much does it cost? The answer is simple: Whatever you make! You will spend whatever your income is. Like "regular" living, there's no way to put a definite price tag on full-time RVing. It is a very democratic lifestyle—it allows rich people and poor people and everything in between. I've talked with people who were getting by on a few hundred dollars a month, and I've talked to people with unlimited bank accounts. I'm fully convinced that you can do it on whatever you make (assuming that you make *something*). Just as in regular life, some people live luxuriously and lavishly whether in a house or RVing with million-dollar rigs and pockets deep enough to handle any expense. On the other hand, there are those with very modest incomes who just got by in regular life who live on the road with inexpensive RVs and just getting by.

The Full-timing Rig and the "Big Four" Budget Factors

The major cost of fulltiming is the rig itself. Most fulltimers already have their rig before they take up the lifestyle. Others buy it with the proceeds from the sale of their houses. Whatever the source, I strongly suggest that the rig be paid for before you start life on the road.

The cost of fulltiming can be geared to almost any financial level by controlling the "Big Four" budget items:

1. How far you travel
2. Where you stay
3. What you eat
4. What you spend that you didn't have to

These are all controllable factors—you directly control each of them; however, there are other factors that you less control over, like medical care, insurance, and vehicle repairs.

I won't presume to present a sample budget. There are just too many variables as well as the fact that most people simply don't use formal budgets. People of "full-timing age" have usually developed patterns of spending over the years that fit their incomes, and they simply jockey the amounts around a bit to fit their new incomes and lifestyle. But I do emphasize that, in the jockeying, you need to take into special consideration the "Big Four" cost factors when you are trying to achieve a balance between what you've got and what you want.

The Cost of the Rig

Obviously, you can spend any amount of money on an RV—ranging from a few thousand dollars to well over a million. In fact, looking out my window as I write this, five spaces away and directly in my view is a converted Prevost bus that cost someone the latter figure. Right down the row is a small trailer towed by an older-model truck with a combined value of just a few thousand dollars. Yet both owners are enjoying the same kind of hookups, the same amenities of the park, and the same camaraderie of other RVers. And the 85-degree sun is beaming exactly the same on each party! Whether or not they are fulltiming, I don't know, but my illustration shows that the rig's use and the enjoyment by their owners is the same regardless of how much their rigs cost.

You don't have to have any particular type of RV or one of any particular value. You buy what you want if you have deep pockets; you buy what you can *afford* if you're like most of us.

Something you should bear in mind regarding the size and value of the rig you choose is that licenses, insurance premiums, and operating costs are directly related to those factors. Ask yourself if you want the long-term costs of whatever RV you choose. In the same vein, consider carefully the financial impact of monthly payments if you start fulltiming with a financed rig.

How Far You Travel

A wise RVer once made this interesting observation: Only engines that are running burn fuel. Very simply, since fuel costs are controlled entirely by much the engine is run, fulltimers have a great opportunity to keep fuel costs down by not driving very much. On the other hand, if they don't mind high fuel bills, they can drive as much as they wish. We know people who drive very few miles each year; they find places they like and settle in for months at a time. And we know people who drive over 25,000 miles a year. In fact, we used to do that when we were giving seminars at RV shows. According to the statistics of experts, the average motorhome owner drives around 10, 000 miles per year.

With fuel costs at this time (February 2003) averaging around $1.70 per gallon (and rising quickly), a motorhome or a tow vehicle giving eight or ten miles per gallon costs from twenty-one cents to seventeen cents per mile for fuel alone. Going 1,000 miles means a significant cost. If you drive 1,000 miles at ten miles per gallon, your fuel cost will be $170; if you drive only 500 miles, that cost will be only $85. If you sit in one place, your fuel cost will be *zero*.

Although these costs can be sobering, the good news is that *you*, the driver, has complete control over how many miles you go; therefore, if you want to cut costs, cut miles driven. That might not be the way you want to do it, but if you have to cut expenses, that is an option you have. Actually, cutting back on the miles can be a good thing. One of the major objectives of fulltiming is to see things, so limiting miles on the road where all you see is road and traffic and increasing time parked gives more time to "smell the roses." Maybe this formula is true: *The enjoyment of fulltiming increases in direct proportion to decreases in the miles driven.*

Other than not driving as much, there are a couple of other ways to soften the blows at the fuel pumps: Get a smaller, lightweight rig and shop fuel prices carefully.

The first of those options is usually not acceptable to most fulltimers since the fact that their rig is their home means that more room is preferable. However, many fulltimers have opted for rigs in mid- to upper-20s sizes for purposes other than fuel economy. They want to be able to take more of the "blue" roads and use campgrounds that large rigs can't comfortable and safely use. Indeed, if you prefer the relatively primitive public campgrounds to fancy resorts, a small rig might be required.

Saving at the Pumps

All gas prices are not equal. That's a fact that anyone who has traveled around the country knows. When you are squirting a gallon of gas into your engine every eight miles, a few cents per gallon makes a difference in a tank-load. Many motorhomes have 100-gallon fuel tanks and trucks with auxiliary fuel tanks almost match that, so a fill-up means savings in dollars, not cents.

Here are some steps I suggest in buying fuel:

1. Plan on stopping in a city or town. As a rule, but certainly not always, the more isolated a station is, the higher the price.
2. Sometimes it pays to get away from the major offramps from freeways. I've noted that in some towns with few offramps, fuel is higher at the first stations than the ones down the street.
3. Always note prices at two or three stations before pulling in. It hurts to discover that fuel is a dime a gallon less just a few blocks or miles down the road.
4. Keep a record of towns or states where fuel is regularly priced lower, and plan fuel stops there when possible.
5. Stop at the big chain truck stops where you know that fuel is regularly priced lower than competitors.
6. Pay cash if there is a difference in cash and credit prices. Often fuel is five cents per gallon less with cash, so, even if you have to use an ATM card and pay a couple of bucks for the privilege, that's better than paying four dollars extra on a credit card.

Where You Stay

A very important means of keeping your budget trimmed is to spend as little as possible for places to stay at night. Space rental at campgrounds and RV parks can range up to well over $50 a night, although a figure of $25 is more common. At $50 a night, you would spend $1500 in a month. But even at $25 a night, the total bill would be $750 for 30 days. On the other hand, you might spend all those nights at places where there is no charge. Those spaces will differ widely in the accommodations you will have, but it can be done. My point is that you have a great variety of options when it comes to settling in for the night as you travel.

To a great extent, you'll get what you pay for in campgrounds. As you travel, you'll see signs along highways advertising campgrounds. Some quote prices that are quite low and, upon utilizing those places, you'll usually find that their service level is also quite low. If a price is half the average, you shouldn't expect much. On the other hand, if you are just stopping for the night, you may not be interested in swimming pools, clubhouses, and hot tubs. In that case, it makes little difference what amenities are provided as long as the hookups you need function well. I've often said, "When you pull the drapes and settle in for the night, it doesn't make any difference what is outside as long as it is safe and quiet."

To plan for campgrounds that fit into your travels and budget, you need a campground guide. The two major books are published by Trailer Life and Woodalls. Both list all the campgrounds and RV parks in the United States and Canada (some of the major parks in Mexico are also listed). Information is provided about where they are, what their services are, and how much they cost, along with evaluations of their quality. By planning well, you can select your destinations and your costs before you get there.

There are several ways to bring campground fees down. The first is to join the Good Sam Club, FMCA, Escapees, or other club that entitles members to discounts at cooperating parks. Usually that discount is 10%. However, there are clubs that enable members to save considerably more; for example, Passport America has a program that reduces prices by 50% at member parks that belong to their association. New programs come (and some go) all the time, so it behooves RVers to keep abreast of discount opportunities.

Nearly all campgrounds have reduced rates for extended periods. For example, the weekly rate is lower per day than the daily rate; the monthly rate is considerably less per day than the weekly or daily rate; and the annual rate is much less. The point is that if you plan your travels to spend more time in fewer places, your accommodations costs will come down.

Memberships campgrounds offer programs that *can* (note that I did not say *will*) reduce your space costs and definitely should be investigated. (See Chapter 15, "Should I Join a Membership Campground?")

What You Eat

We all have to eat—that is a given. However, what you eat and where you eat it can make a tremendous difference in your pocketbook. For example, eating hamburger cooked on a grill outside your RV is one thing (and price), but eating steak at a fine restaurant is something else. Even eating a hamburger at a restaurant versus eating one cooked at your RV makes a huge difference in price. The point is simply that if you eat out a lot, your food bill for the month is going to be a lot bigger.

I make a distinction between *eating out* and *dining out*. In the latter, you might go to a grand restaurant, be seated by a maitre d' at an elegantly set table, start with cocktails and appetizers, have a steak and lobster, a bottle of wine, a flaming dessert, and finally an after-dinner drink—which will be followed by another sizzling item—a bill that would support a couple eating at home for a month. That's *dining out*.

On the other hand, that same couple can drop in at Denny's and get a reasonable five-course dinner from the senior's menu, pay with a twenty-dollar bill, and get enough change to pick up a bottle of Ripple on the way home for that after-dinner drink. Now, that's eating out.

Denny's might never win awards for fine dining, but you can count on them to provide a full meal for a very modest price. They aren't alone. There are family restaurants with modest prices in every town.

Many good restaurants have "early-bird specials" that are considerably reduced from regular prices, but you have to eat early—usually by five o'clock (sometimes six).

And, a final tip, if you are accustomed to a glass of wine or other kind of "nip" before dining, have it at home before you go (assuming you aren't the driver). A bottle of wine in a restaurant almost invariably costs three times what it does in a store and cocktails are equally marked up.

What You Spend That You Didn't Have To

Whether it's for ourselves or gifts for others, we all spend money on things that are nonessentials. Some are fairly big-ticket items—satellite TVs, computers, cameras, etc.—and others are minor—gifts, souvenirs, movies, even this book. The point is that we don't have to have these things. But we want them, so a certain portion of our income is spent on things that we could do without. Together, they all add up, so if you want to RV on a modest budget, you'll have to watch carefully that you don't buy too many things that you really don't have to.

Most of us spend a great deal of money on nonessentials, but we have become so accustomed to some of them that we wouldn't think of being without them as long as we have the money to pay for them.

The Total Cost of Fulltiming

"How much income do I need to go fulltiming?" That's a question I get regularly, especially from younger couples who don't have a fixed retirement income on which to depend.

I can't give them a specific number simply because there is no such number. It's like trying to answer the question for "regular" people who live "regular" lives. The reality is that the figure varies enormously. Perhaps my glib response, "Whatever you make," isn't too far off the mark.

Don't most people for much of their lives spend whatever their pay-check is? People who make $2,000 a month usually spend $2,000 a month; people who make $5,000, spend $5,000, and so on. It's the same with RVers. Whatever income you have, you probably spend. Of course, there are always people who put away some—even in retirement—for a "rainy day." But, generally, most people spend the majority of what they make as they go along.

I have been interviewing fulltimers for many years, and I have gleaned some information about their habits, including their incomes and spending. In the 1990s, I noted that those amounts increased considerably. As the present generation (the boomers) enters the full-timing lifestyle, they bring with them a record of higher earnings and higher retirement incomes. Probably the average fulltimer is making and spending 50% more than the preceding generation. I've seen a median full-timing income increase from around $1,500 in the late 1980s to something closer to double that in the early 2000s. The reason is that many couples are both bringing in substantial incomes, thereby making the family income quite large. In fact, some of my recent surveys show that many full-timing couples have annual incomes over $75,000 a year.

The fact that some fulltimers have large incomes shouldn't deter people with lesser amounts from going. Most fulltimers will still be able to enjoy the lifestyle with incomes closer to what they made in "regular" life. You don't have to have a lot of money to enjoy some of the benefits of life on the road. Just as the price of the rig doesn't determine how happy one will be, the same principle applies to incomes. Nature's bounty, for example, is generally free. The elation and satisfaction of seeing Yellowstone Falls is no greater for the rich man that for one who is poor; the breakers on the Oregon coast pound no louder or higher for the couple with a million-dollar motorhome than one with a homemade camper on an old truck. Maybe the wealthier people can dine out regularly on fancy foods, but they can't enjoy their dinners any more than people who roast wieners over a campfire at a campsite by a mountain stream. In short, whether or not you take up fulltiming doesn't have to depend on your finances, but how you do it definitely does.

CHAPTER NINETEEN

How Do I Choose a Full-timing Rig?

The perspective from which one chooses a full-timing rig may differ drastically from the perspective one uses in selecting a rig for recreational use. In the latter case, you are seeking temporary shelter away from home during vacations; in the former, the object of your search is the *home* that must provide all the functions of the house you give up to take to the road. Unlike recreational use, which may involve inconveniences that can be overlooked because they are of short duration, fulltiming means 365 days a year in that motorhome or trailer—be it convenient or inconvenient, comfortable or uncomfortable, practical or impractical, loved or hated. If you fail to properly judge your needs when purchasing a full-time rig, you may have nagging regrets that you didn't make a wiser choice before handing over your money.

Some Rules for Choosing an RV

The saying "different strokes for different folks" is nowhere more meaningful than with people who are buying RVs that will serve as their homes. Even though there is a general lifestyle labeled *fulltiming*, the fact is that there are many variations on how one lives full time in an RV. Those variations make it difficult, even impossible, to designate one size, one floorplan, one style as the perfect rig. That perfection has to be achieved within the limitations and requirements individuals impose upon themselves with their personal needs and wants.

However, there are some general rules I believe to be quite valid, regardless of one's personal preferences. My rules don't provide specifics, but, hopefully, they will provide some basis for judgments.

Size

With few exceptions, full-timing rigs are relatively large if the people who live in them have a choice. Generally, that means something over 30 feet, more likely, over 35 feet. In fact, until the advent of slide-outs, 40-footers were the size of choice for most fulltimers. However, with two or more slide-outs, shorter rigs have become more popular.

My "size rule" is: *Buy as large as you want, that is, what appeals most to you in terms of livability, as long as there is no valid reason you shouldn't buy something that large.* For example, you might want a 40-footer, but you know it won't be practical for traveling on high, curvy, narrow roads where you plan to spend a lot of time traveling for fishing. Or you might want to make extensive use of public parks, some of which have size limits. Or you might be terrified to drive a rig 40 feet long. No doubt you could, but if doing so would give you white knuckles every time you got behind the wheel, your trips would make you miserable. That's certainly is a good reason not to have a 40-footer. Another obvious reason is that larger rigs cost more, and you might not have the wherewithal to pay for the huge one that you want.

But, if you really want a large rig and you can't come up with any reason not to buy one, go for it. Always remember when you are shopping that this is going to be your *home*. It's where you are going to live, and you should plan to live comfortably.

Incidentally, you very seldom see or hear of a fulltimer complaining that their rig is too big, but a lot of them regret that they got one too little. Many end up trading up for larger ones, but practically never trade down for shorter ones.

Quality

Just as I can't recall hearing many complaints about having a rig that is too big, I can't recall ever hearing anyone complaining about the quality of the rig they have being too good. On the other hand, I've heard many disappointed owners complain about the "junk" they had bought. A problem is that people have the contradictory dilemma of wanting a *cheap price* with *high quality*. Unfortunately, the two don't ordinarily go together, and the result is that some RV buyers end up with the former without the latter. The general rule that "you get what you pay for" often describes the situation with RV buyers. If a company puts out a line of motorhomes that range in price from $100,000 up to a million dollars, the probability is that the more expensive rigs are of a better overall quality than those that are less expensive. That doesn't always hold true, but, in general, it does.

My point is: Don't deceive yourself or let a salesperson deceive you into believing that the bottom of the line is as good as the top. When you're shopping for the rig that is going to be your home for the foreseeable future, you want to do it right the first time.

Options

When it comes to the options that are available on an RV, my basic rule is: *Get every option offered unless there's a reason not to.* Examples of reasons not to include an option would be: If you never watch TV in bed, don't get a TV in the bedroom; if leveling jacks that cost $4,000 bust your budget, don't get them; if you prefer cloth to leather, don't get leather upholstery.

The notion that one should skip some options now and add them later is not a good one. Most options are better installed and lower priced if they are added during the manufacturing process. For example, imagine the job of installing leveling jacks under the motorhome—welding, boring, wiring, etc.—in a very limited space with all the stuff that is in the way. Compare that with making an installation when the chassis is bare rails and accessible from any angle.

I don't suggest that you should buy every option that is offered—just those that you *want*.

Livability

The best advice I can give you in selecting an RV for full-time use is to find what you think you want, but, before you buy it, give it a "livability test." Do a pretend live-in. Go through each room doing what you expect to be normally doing there.

After the evening meal, nearly everyone goes to the living room or den and sits for several hours. Dad has *his* chair and Mom has *her* place. Find those places in the RV you think you might be living in and sit. After all, you're going to be spending a lot of your life there reading or watching TV. Find out now how comfortable or uncomfortable the situation is and how you would feel after three hours sitting there. It's a little late to discover on your first trip that your chair puts kinks in your back or the TV is not well located from your angle.

In the kitchen, do a mock cooking session. Go through all the motions required to make an apple pie. Where are the apples stored?

The spices and other ingredients that go in an apple pie? The pie plate and rolling pin? Do you have enough room to roll out the dough? Try to visualize all the things you will want in your kitchen in places—drawers, cabinets, and shelves. Do you have places for everything?

Then go to the bedroom. Theoretically, you will spend a third of your life in bed. Is it comfortable? Are the lights in the right places? Do you have adequate closet and drawer space?

Finally, the bathroom. Stand in the shower and make the motions you normally make when showering. Is the medicine cabinet large enough for your needs? Is there plenty of counter space around the lavatory for your "stuff?" Sit on the commode. Does its location suit you?

Although you don't live in it, your outside storage capability has a lot to do with your livability of the unit. That's where you carry all the stuff you need to maintain a normal existence on the road. You need to know the carrying capacity both in terms of space and weight.

In short, find out the good and the bad before you buy. You're need to know insofar as possible whether or not each part of the motorhome or trailer suits your needs before you start spending 365 days a year in it. A bells-and-whistles-laden, gorgeous motorhome with a stunning paint job could prove quite unsatisfactory if it is uncomfortable and impractical for long-term use.

The Final Decision

Listen to all suggestions and reasons other people give you for getting certain sizes, floorplans, options, and styles, but make the final decisions yourselves. Make that decision alone (the couple) without salespeople, Uncle Mortimer, and good buddy Henry. Their personal preferences are not necessary for your final decision.

I doubt if you will find the "perfect rig." All RVs usually turn out to have some drawbacks along with their many great features. I've long maintained that every decision in choosing an RV is a compromise. You give up one advantage to get another. For example, you might want a washer-dryer, but you have to give up a rather large space that might satisfy some other more important need you have. You have to choose between large size, which gives room and comfort, and short size, which gives maneuverability and adaptability to small campsites. Whether large or small, there are limitations or disadvantages on every size of RV. You just have to decide what is most important to you. And remember, everything is a compromise: You get something, you give something.

Choosing the Right Type of RV

Of the five RV types—motorhomes, travel trailers, fifth-wheel trailers, pickup campers, and folding trailers—only the first three are popular with fulltimers. As to which is best, I can only say that it is up to the individual. Good arguments pro and con on each are possible. However, for the benefit of readers who are undecided, I'll present a few points they might consider in choosing an RV type.

Travel Trailers

The travel trailer is a popular full-timing rig. Generally it is the least expensive way to go compared to a motorhome or fifth-wheel. And it is the least expensive to operate and maintain. If you already have a tow rig, you can get into a home-for-the-road quite inexpensively. If you have to buy the tow truck or other large vehicle capable of pulling a large trailer, you can still stay well under the price of a comparable size motorhome or fifth wheel. And, from a maintenance and repair standpoint, a trailer has fewer things to break or malfunction. Added to that is the fact that your tow rig probably gives better mileage than the other types of RVs.

Another plus for trailers is that they offer variety in floorplans with choices of front kitchens, front living rooms, or front bedrooms.

A basic minus for trailers is the setup time required for hitching and unhitching and leveling. Also, obviously one has to ride in the tow vehicle with the necessity to stop and go back to the trailer to use the bathroom, get a snack or a drink, or for the co-pilot to take a nap. On a cold, rainy day, that can be inconvenient and uncomfortable. However, on the other hand, getting out for a stretch regularly is a good idea.

Fifth-Wheels

Fifth-wheel trailers are very popular with fulltimers, primarily because of their roominess and diversity of floor plans. Nearly all have slide-outs—some as many as four—that make them quite large and comfortable. Fulltimers who spend most of their time parked often opt for the largest ones—40-footers.

Fifth-wheels come with a variety of floorplans; however, almost invariably the bedroom and bath are up front in the part that overhangs the truck bed. In their early years, bedrooms had low ceilings and were cramped, but, nowadays, they have plenty of headroom. The addition of two slide-outs in the bedroom makes it spacious and comfortable. With two more slide-outs, living–dining areas contain many of the features found in most houses—lots of storage area, comfortable chairs, large entertainment center, dining table with four chairs, and, in many, computer desks.

From a safety standpoint, the fifth-wheel is very stable to tow. Unlike travel trailers, they are much less susceptible to jackknifing when the tow vehicle swerves sharply. Many fifth-wheels have huge storage compartments that are easily accessed, which increases their usefulness for fulltimers. In that storage area, owners who like to boondock often have generators installed, which along with solar panels, make their rigs independent of shore power.

Although fifth-wheels have a lot going for them, there are some drawbacks. One is that due to the size and weight of some of the larger models, it takes very powerful trucks to pull them. In fact, a whole new generation of "tow rigs" cropped up in the 1990s—medium-duty diesel trucks converted specifically for fifth-wheel towing. Although they are wonderful, powerful tow rigs, many with interiors that border on elegance, they are big, heavy, and expensive. But there are other choices for larger, powerful tow rigs offered by conventional Detroit automobile manufacturers.

As with travel trailers, using a fifth-wheel means that when you're on the road, you are riding in a truck that you must stop and get out of to use any of the facilities of the trailer.

Motorhomes

Motorhomes offer the greatest variety in sub-types: Class As, Class Bs, and Class Cs. Generally, fulltimers opt for Class As because of the room they offer both for living and for storage.

Undoubtedly the most popular feature of motorhomes is you're always inside it, whether driving down the road or using it as a home in a campground. Viewing the world through a motorhome's huge windshield is great, but, a better feature is that passengers can enjoy many of its "living features" as they travel—use the bathroom, take a nap, fix a snack, and move about (one should always be aware that being unbuckled from your seat isn't the safest way to travel).

When we are rushing to get from Point A to Point B, as our schedule sometimes demands, while traveling, Margie often fixes me a snack to eat or a soft drink to sip as I drive. (I know safety freaks will take issue with this activity, but we've been doing it for thirty years and don't intend to quit now.)

The basement feature on most motorhomes today became popular in the 1980s and the slide-out in the 1990s. Now nearly all motorhomes have both, which makes motorhomes spacious while providing storage for lots of "stuff."

For most old-timer motorhomers, the greatest option on a motorhome is leveling jacks. Back in the "olden days," we had to carry lots of blocks to pull up on to level up (trailerists still have to do that). With four wheels to level, it was a real job at times. Now all you have to do is push a button and four jacks come down and a computer takes over. Within seconds, your rig is perfectly level and all you had to do was push a button. Of course, there's a compromise that goes with those jacks—like $4,000!

On the minus side, motorhomes are usually the most expensive way to go. Prices for motorhomes can run up to astronomical numbers, up to well over a million dollars. However, major manufacturers have lines that compare favorably with the combined prices of similar size fifth-wheels and tow rigs. Also, operating and repair costs are usually higher than on pull units. The fact that motorhomes are a very complicated melding of what is essentially a truck chassis with a house opens the door for many kinds of mechanical and electrical troubles not common to trailers.

Your Choice

The wisest choice generally is determined partly by preference and partly by use. For example, if you wish to travel extensively—here today, gone tomorrow—you can't beat a motorhome. The ease of setting up gives it quite an edge over trailers if you have to do it nearly every night. However, if your normal pattern is to move only a few times a year, ease of setup is no big factor. Floor space and livability may be the most important features, which might make a fifth-wheel more practical. Or the cost might figure prominently in your decision, in which case a travel trailer might be the best choice.

In short, I can't tell you what would be best for you. I can only advise that you picture carefully how you expect to use the rig, think carefully how a potential choice that you are considering fits that picture, and make your own conclusion as to what is best for you.

And bear this in mind: The bad news is that the odds you will choose the "perfect rig" are about the same as those for winning the lottery. The good news is that no matter what your choice is, you will probably learn to live with its drawbacks and enjoy it immensely.

CHAPTER TWENTY

How Do I Pick Up Extra Bucks?

Most fulltimers are retired. That means no more punching a time clock five days a week. It also means no more paychecks on Friday!

As a rule, people who have opted for a life on the road have regular incomes, in most cases Social Security, which is often supplemented with company retirement benefits and personal savings or investments. However, it isn't uncommon for fulltimers to want or need to pick up extra dollars as they travel. Fortunately, there are many employment niches into which they can fit themselves.

The amount you move determines to a great extent what some of the job opportunities are. Some fulltimers want to move often, while others don't mind stopping for extended periods of time. If you are one who likes to travel a lot, you must find something that doesn't depend on your being in a particular place. On the other hand, if you are a snowbird who likes to settle in for the winter somewhere in the Sun Belt and in a cool summer location in the north, some different employment doors open.

A trend that is increasing in popularity is companies hiring older people because they are better, more responsible workers than younger people in certain jobs. In snowbird areas where many temporary employees are necessary to handle the increase in business during the season, older folks can often be found sacking groceries and doing other work generally done by teenagers.

The following suggestions represent only a few of the major opportunities job seekers have and they are not in any ranked order.

Workamping

Since the advent of the publication of *Workamper News* (available at www.lifeonwheels.com), it has become a relatively simple matter for fulltimers who want temporary employment to get jobs in campgrounds. *Workamper News* is basically a classified ad site that brings together campgrounds that need personnel with people who want to work in campgrounds. There are hundreds of openings listed for clerical and maintenance workers, generally in the Sun Belt during the winter and the north during the summer. Remuneration for most jobs isn't large, but usually includes a space. Some of the jobs are for permanent personnel so those who are looking for a new career will find some great opportunities, often in large, resort parks. Besides their classified ads in the *Workamper News*, the publishing company offers "job fairs" at both ends of the country—Florida and Arizona.

For those who like real camping, many public parks hire seasonal help: U.S. Forest Service, Corps of Engineers, state parks, even some county and city campgrounds. Often the job pays little or no cash, but does provide a space with full hookups and the hours are not long. Sometimes there are openings for jobs that provide paychecks at concessions in parks where one member of the couple can work for money while the other works for a space.

People with special skills or trades—carpenters, electricians, plumbers, mechanics (particularly RV technicians)—can usually find temporary work when they want it. One couple we met takes inventory for various kinds of businesses. The couple simply sign up with the branch agencies that are in most cities and work when they want to. I've known of several men who belonged to trade unions who traveled and checked into local union halls when they found a place they wanted to visit for a while. We've met ladies who were registered nurses who had no problem in finding work as they traveled. Good salespeople can always find temporary work selling RVs in snowbird areas during their seasons. I've met several experts who work more or less full time on their computers as they travel and simply e-mail in their product. I'm in that category because I write wherever I am and e-mail my articles.

I think the neatest part-time job I've ever run on to was the fellow in the Florida Keys who spent his winters at a pleasant RV park and fished all day. He had a nice boat and was apparently a good fisherman. Every day, he brought his catch back to the dock at the park, and people came from all sides to buy his fresh fish. We saw him take in many dollars while we were there, including some of ours. That fellow really knew how to mix a business with pleasure.

In another very unique case, I learned about an attractive young woman who parked her motorhome at a rest area on I-8 between Yuma and Gila Bend in southern Arizona and set up business. Her *modus operandi* was to beam smiles at men without female companions, invite them in for coffee, tell a tale of woe, and in apparent desperation, offer her "personal attentions" for "gas money" to get her back to her home several states away. (Don't ask me how I know about this case, and I'm certainly not recommending this "job.")

In short, opportunities for fulltimers to trade know-how or muscle power for extra cash are almost unlimited. Add a little job-hunting effort, and you'll probably find a nice niche for yourself.

Sell a Product

I've run across several enterprising fulltimers who were in effect simply "in business." A couple we met a while back had a route that they serviced by selling packages of almonds. They purchased the almonds wholesale in bulk, repacked them in small plastic bags, and created a product that they marketed as snack food in service stations and other small retail outlets,

At every RV show and at large rallies, you will see fulltimers selling all kinds of products. Some have products small enough to carry in cargo bays of their motorhomes or trailers; some motorhomers pull cargo trailers in which they have room for both their cars and their merchandise. Some specialize in products that appeal primarily to other RVers while others sell items that appeal to a wider market. In nearly all RV parks and rallies, there will be people selling recognized products like Amway and Mary Kay cosmetics. The fact is, the list of items that one can buy to resell is almost endless.

Many fulltimers have an artistic talent that can be used to create income. Once we were parked next to a fellow in a campground who was creating beautiful brass art works at his picnic table. He towed a travel trailer behind a van in which he carried all his raw materials and tools. In a discussion with him, I found that he traveled up and down the East Coast exhibiting and selling his creations at shopping mall art shows.

Quartzsite, Arizona, is the epitome of swap meets involving RVers. Although the initial meetings there over a quarter of a century ago were geared to rockhounds, it has developed into a major event that draws hundreds of thousands of RVers every winter who are offered everything from fossilized dinosaur dung to half-million-dollar motorhomes. Many of the merchants are RVers who do business right in front of their parked RVs that are hooked up to utilities. Most have merchandise purchased for resale, but some offer their artistic creations—paintings, woodcarvings, sculptures, ceramics, and so forth.

I've seen some unusual ways of picking up extra dollars on the road, but I think one that tops all was the fellow who was an itinerant clown. His converted bus contained not only living quarters for a couple, but a barn for animals in the rear. His act included a goat, so he carried two—one for a spare.

Musically talented snowbirds are in great demand in the large snowbird roosts. Nearly every large park holds dances, so small bands that play "the oldies" can easily work two or three nights a week. Although their gigs won't make them rich, they can pick up extra bucks while having a good time themselves.

The list of ideas for making extra dollars while you travel full time is endless. For some ideas, I suggest you try book titles offered in the bookstore at www.lifeonwheels.com.

CHAPTER TWENTY-ONE

How Do I Choose a Home Base?

One of the interesting paradoxes of fulltiming is that you can give up your job, your home, your friends and neighbors, and your city, but you can't give up a *state*. In fact, even though you don't expect to live anywhere, you must claim an address in a state. Why? Because you must have two licenses—driver's and vehicle—and they are issued only by states to *residents* of those states. Of course there are other reasons to claim residence (e.g., voting), but they are optional; those licenses aren't.

Choosing the Right State

Although as an American citizen you have the right to be a resident of any state, you must conform to a state's requirements for residence. In most states, a requirement is a physical address as your domicile. In no case does a state require ownership of property—just an address. A few states allow post-office boxes to meet the address requirement, but they are becoming fewer.

Since a fulltimer doesn't actually reside anywhere permanently, a logical question all prospective fulltimers ask is: How do I meet the residence requirement somewhere in order to get the necessary licenses? And therein lies both a legal and possibly moral question. You have to claim an address *somewhere* because you have to have those licenses. But if you claim an address where you don't really live, isn't that a violation of law? Well, technically it could be, but, since I'm not a lawyer, I don't give legal advice. Certainly it would be a falsehood to claim residence in a state where you don't live, so wouldn't that be a lie? That's a moral question and, since I'm not a preacher, I don't give moral advice. However, I can state unequivocally that *you have to claim an address somewhere in some state.* The good news is that regardless of the state you obtain an address in, that state will welcome you as long as you abide by all the laws of that state. That's where it becomes vital that you choose a state where the laws best suit your particular situation. And generally the biggest concern is how those laws affect your pocketbook.

State Taxes

Every states levies taxes, but they vary enormously and affect individuals according to their income, purchases, vehicles, real estate, and certain other possessions. Income tax, sales tax, licenses and registrations, and property taxes (real and personal) are factors that every fulltimer should consider when choosing a state for claiming residence. Every year one or more of the finance-oriented magazines publishes a list of the various taxes in all fifty states and ranks them in order from high to low in terms of their cost to taxpayers.

How much you make, how much you buy, the value, size, or weight of your vehicles, real estate you own, and, in some states, various personal possessions determine how much you will have to pay out every year in taxes. As representatives of all social and economic levels of our society, fulltimers who are interested in saving money need to compare the tax laws of several "full-timer-friendly" states and see which one best fits their needs. Choosing the right state can make a difference of thousands of dollars every year to a fulltimer

Some states have no income tax; in others, that tax is very high. Some states have no sales tax; in others, it ranges up to nearly 10%. Some states have very low cost vehicle licenses; in others, licenses or other special fees can make annual fees huge. Although there are fifty sets of state laws, those of only a few states greatly affect the average RVer. I'll discuss a few of them with illustrations of how they can affect individual pocketbooks.

If you frequently buy big-ticket items such as new RVs, automobiles, or boats, or generally spend a lot of money, you might consider a state with no sales tax (at present, Delaware, Montana, New Hampshire, and Oregon). As with state income taxes, the amounts levied in sales tax vary enormously from state to state. In fact, local sales taxes imposed by other jurisdictions—county or city—cause rates to vary within states. Snowbirds choosing a place in which to spend several winter months can be particularly affected by sales taxes on purchases of things that everyone has to buy: food, clothing, and shelter. The difference between 8% and no percent in four or five months of purchases makes a considerable difference in a budget. For example, a $100,000 motorhome purchased in Oregon will cost only $100,000 for residents of that state, but it will cost residents of California or Washington over $108,000.

Another form of taxation is the licensing of vehicles. Again, states vary enormously in those costs. In some states, that license is a fixed cost for a motorhome or trailer regardless of size, weight, or value and can be quite minimal. In other states, license rates are determined by how much the rig weighs or what its value is, and the costs can be very high. You should note that vehicle license fees are easy targets for state officials to change—invariably upward—as well as other fees associated with vehicles.

Since everyone has to buy vehicle licenses every year, the pocketbook-impact at license renewal time can be significantly different in different

states. For example, the purchaser of a new $100,000 motorhome might
pay over $1,000 for a first-year license in a state that bases fees on a per-
centage of a vehicle's value, but the buyer of that rig in a state with very
low license fees might pay under $100. Although the cost decreases annu-
ally in some states, in a ten-year period, an RV owner might pay thousands of dollars more than an owner domiciled in a state with very low
fees. In short, vehicle license prices should be looked at by every fulltimer
when choosing a state in which to claim residence. You also need to be
aware that some states assess a special tax on RVs based on their value.

In the U.S., we have the right to be residents of whatever state we
choose. None are perfect, but there's a best state for every pocketbook.

State Income Tax

A few states do not have a state income tax (at present, Alaska, New
Hampshire, Florida, Nevada, Oregon, South Dakota, Texas, and Washington). All others do, and that tax varies enormously from state to state.
By choosing one of the no-income-tax states, fulltimers with taxable
incomes can save hundreds, even thousands of dollars every year on
income taxes. However, all states obtain revenues somewhere, so those
with no income tax often have high sales, real estate, or personal property taxes. For people with low taxable incomes, factors other than
income should determine the choice of a state of residence.

Here's an example of the effect of being a resident in the "right" state:
If you pay $4,000 federal income tax (everyone pays federal income tax
regardless of the state they live in), your state income tax would be
$1,000 in a state in which the state income tax is 25% of what you pay
in federal taxes. Several states use a percentage of the federal tax as a
basis for determining their income taxes.

Popular States

Probably more fulltimers claim residence in Texas than any other state, primarily because the Escapees club is based there. Although not all tax factors are the best in that state, some are very good (no state income tax, low license fees), and the fact that it is easy to qualify as a Texas resident by membership in the club is a big plus.

South Dakota is fast becoming a "state of choice" for many fulltimers. No only does it have no state income tax, license fees are reasonable, and the sales tax is relatively low. The fact that it allows a post office box as a legal address has encouraged the establishing of mail-forwarding services.

Final Note

Due to the fact that states regularly change their laws pertaining to taxes, it is very important that when you think you have the right state for your needs that you contact the appropriate agencies in that state and verify the present situation. It is doubtful that there will be changes in the status of those states with no income tax, but license fees and sales taxes are fair game for increases in most states.

CHAPTER TWENTY-TWO

Can I Go Home Again?

Making the decision to become a fulltimer can be very difficult. The prospect of giving up one's home, family, familiar people, places, things, and comfortable routines most of us develop is indeed sobering. It should be—as any major change in a family's way of doing things should be. I'm among the first and loudest to recommend great care in making the decision. But I'm equally quick to point out that a decision to take up fulltiming isn't an ironclad, lifetime contract. You can start when you want and you can quit when you want. And contrary to the famous and oft-quoted claim that "you can't go home again," I reply, "Not only can you go home again, most fulltimers at some point in their lives do plant roots again."

Why RVers Give Up Fulltiming

Fulltimers return to "normal" living for many reasons. Unfortunately, as they get older, ill health is often the determining factor. Or just plain old age and the deterioration of the human body demand a more settled life, one close to particular doctors or health-care facilities. Sometimes advancing age or ill health brings with the need to be close to family, especially children. Advancing age doesn't necessarily mean the end of RVing. I'm aware of many instances in which the "old folks" moved into parks near their children or even on land owned by those children and still lived basically independent lives in their own RVs.

Even if our health doesn't give out on us, eventually Mother Nature (or the law) tells us that we can't handle our big rigs properly or safely, and we have to give them up. I just hope I'm smart enough to recognize that time and do it of my own accord. I suspect that most of us will recognize the problem when we find ourselves having difficulties in making the fast and correct decisions necessary as pilots of big RVs. (Actually, I don't have to worry about making that decision—Margie will make it for me.)

Although many fulltimers are more or less forced to stop living on the road for physical or other problems, most simply give it up because they want to. Some discover marvelous places where the temptation to stay indefinitely is irresistible; others simply tire of being on the go and living in limited spaces. In short, most fulltimers have nothing to keep them from giving up that lifestyle any time they want to.

Another Choice: Park Models

Many of my former full-timing friends have roots again but still retain many of the benefits and attributes of their former lifestyle. They have purchased spaces in condo or co-op RV parks, or they lease them on an annual basis. Many have purchased park-model trailers that provide some of the features of small houses or mobile homes. Although the trailers have only 400 square feet of floor space, many owners add on rooms to increase living space to twice that.

The special attraction of living in a park model is that by living in RV parks (as opposed to mobile-home parks), the ambiance is more like the RV lifestyle. Most of the large resort parks offer wonderful amenities—swimming pools, hot tubs, ballrooms, craft shops, pool rooms, tennis courts, some even have golf courses, and many offer a multitude of entertainments and organized activities. It's the better of two worlds in a way—you have relatively large living quarters in a fun-oriented environment that is secure and relatively inexpensive.

Many park-model owners keep their RVs, which they have available for travel any time the mood strikes them. When they tire of being at home, they simply lock the doors of their park trailers, leave them within the security of walls or fences, and head out to new adventures. The park model is a nice compromise between living in a motorhome or trailer and living in a house—a great deal of comfort for a lot less responsibility, cost, and work.

Other Options

Although I have talked with many semi-settled former fulltimers who have opted for owning or leasing more or less permanent quarters again, none expressed a desire to go back to exactly what they had before they took up fulltiming. They don't want their old homes and all that went with it. Their general preferences at this point in their lives are for small, easy-to-maintain living spaces that are relatively inexpensive. Condos, townhouses, and apartments are the usual choices, although some want their own houses on their own land.

The point is, if you are holding off from fulltiming because you aren't sure you want to spend the rest of your life living that way, bear in mind that you can go home again any time you choose. However, that return may not be without financial loss, particularly in the sale of your rig and the fact that real estate prices are continually rising.

On the other hand, giving up fulltiming can be an excellent opportunity to readjust to housing needs that are different from those previously required. It could be an opportune time to choose a new locale, perhaps in the Sun Belt or in an area where living costs are relatively low. Empty nesters, as most fulltimers are, have different needs than families and the post–full-timing period is an excellent time to address new issues.

CHAPTER TWENTY-THREE

Where Can I Get More Information?

According to the Recreational Vehicle Industry Association, nearly ten million American families own RVs. Finding adventure and freedom from the comfort of a portable home has become "the thing" for millions of folks. It is a comfortable, easy way for them to realize their dreams.

Until just a few years ago, the only way to get information about RVing was to talk to more experienced people, attend seminars at RV shows, or to read the few published books on the subject. Actually, most people learned the hard way—by experience. However, the picture has changed now and you can learn how to RV properly a more conventional way—by going to college.

From Kindergarten to College for RVers

A modern trend in education has been for college community enrichment departments to offer courses in "everyday life" that appeal to adults. Many of those courses are directed toward folks who wish to develop art or craft skills; others appeal to people who wish to improve their work skills; still others more or less randomly address various, sometimes unique, interests.

Despite the fact that RVing is a recreational activity for millions of folks—for many a full-time way of life—there has been little effort to help those people with quality information about their expensive, time-consuming choice of lifestyle. Although some RVers are perfectly happy to learn everything about RVing from experience, others would prefer to save themselves money and trouble by learning from experts first. However, until very recently, college courses in RVing have been far and few between.

The First Life on Wheels Conference

That condition was changed by the development of the Life on Wheels program at the University of Idaho in 1994. Although the program started with only one class on "Extended-Time RVing," the response was so overwhelming that it became a full-fledged conference the next year with nearly 500 attendees, a number that has continued about the same since. Attendees have come from every state in the United States, Canada, and several foreign countries.

Extension Programs

Following the success of the program in Idaho, extension programs have been developed and are offered at Harrisburg Area Community College, Harrisburg, Pennsylvania; Des Moines Area Community College, Des Moines, Iowa; and Western Kentucky University, Bowling Green, Kentucky.

Seminar Topics

The Life on Wheels program at the University of Idaho includes over 150 different "how-to," "where-to," and "what-to" courses in three categories: (1) *lifestyle*, with subjects such as fulltiming, choosing an RV, packing an RV, membership campgrounds, RV driving lessons, where to get camping and travel information, etc., (2) *technical*, courses such as understanding and maintaining the various systems RVs have, maintaining chassis, improving performance of gas and diesel engines, weight safety, choosing and maintaining tires, etc., and (3) *lifestyle enhancement*, courses relating to such subjects as things that are commonly done by RVers: how to take better photos, how to keep a log or journal, travel with pets, RV cooking, health maintenance, etc. In short, every aspect of RVs and the RV lifestyle is addressed. Various interests and degrees of experience are taken into account including many courses that are for the beginner (over 20% of the attendees are non–RV owners).

Safety

Several seminars address safety issues. The Dick Reed RV Driving School offers both classroom instruction and private driving lessons in the students' own rigs. Sandy and Dave Baleria, both retired law enforcement officers, present several classes relating to personal safety. The RV Safety Education Foundation offers classes in weight and tire safety. "Mac" McCoy, formerly a fire safety training specialist for the state of Oregon, teaches fire safety including real-scenario firefighting.

Expert Instructors

Among the instructors are RVing book authors and magazine writers Joe and Vicki Kieva, Bill Farlow, Sharlene "Charlie" Minshall, Marilyn Abraham and Sandy McGregor, Ron and Barb Hofmeister, and many experts from the RV lifestyle and industry. Some are former university professors; others come from various scientific and technical fields. All are selected for their ability to communicate their skills to other RVers.

Campus Camping at Idaho

Students at the University of Idaho conference live on campus in their RVs during their week-long stay. Thirty-amp power is provided at each RV, water is within hose reach of each rig, and "honey-wagon" service is available. Preconference and evening opportunities to enjoy fun activities are available.

Thousands of students have been enrolled in the various schools. Since it is impossible to take all the courses that are offered in one conference, many students return to get courses they missed the first time. Students receive noncredit certificates of completion when they have attended four conferences.

Special Attraction at Harrisburg

Although all extension-programs are shorter than the Idaho conference, the Harrisburg conference has the added attraction of being immediately followed by one of the largest RV shows in the country, which students may attend free of charge. Thus, students get an opportunity to relate the information they learn in classes directly to all the latest in RVs and RV equipment. Although they are not provided with hookups, students enrolled in the Life on Wheels school dry-camp on the State Farm Complex parking lot.

Beautiful Campus at Des Moines

The Des Moines Area Community College's beautiful campus is sprawling and features ponds with lots of wildlife. Parking-lot camping is free, but there are no services.

An extra-curricular activity is a "farm-style Iowa dinner," which is followed by musical entertainment. The conference is held in the latter part of September.

Kentucky in the Springtime

The conference at Western Kentucky University at Bowling Green occurs in May when the countryside is its most beautiful. Students have the option of dry-camping on the South Campus parking lot or living with full hookups at closeby campgrounds. Many students tag on a trip to nearby Nashville following the conference..

Wannabe Attendees

Approximately 20% of the attendees at Life on Wheels conferences are non–RV owners. Their motto could well be "learn first, spend later" which makes them indeed the smart ones. Many of the seminars are directly aimed at wannabes.

Information about Life on Wheels

For information at any or all conferences, call toll free 1-866-LOW-GOGO (1-866-569-4646), E-mail: Peggy Waterman at peggyw@uidaho.edu or write to: Enrichment Program, University of Idaho, Moscow, ID, 83844.
For detailed information about courses, check www.lifeonwheels.com.

CHAPTER TWENTY-FOUR

When Should I Start?

The decision to go fulltiming is one of life's "big ones." Only in a few other instances will the average person have the opportunity to choose a new direction for his or her life that will have the impact this one does. I have several suggestions that you should bear in mind when you are making this choice.

Make the Decision Together

It is absolutely crucial both husband and wife make the decision jointly (assuming your are a couple), and that you are both in agreement. I can't imagine anything more horrible than for a couple to sell their home, give up most of their possessions, leave their kids and grandkids, and take up a nomadic life if one of the parties is totally against it. I'm sure than in many cases one or both persons may have some misgivings about the change, but there's an enormous difference between "some misgivings" and "totally against." Most people who get into the full-timing lifestyle have some concerns about the future, but, like the sensible people they are, they weigh the pros and cons and generally come up with the right decision.

Set a Time

There are some people who never seem to be able to make up their minds. They think about fulltiming, they talk about it to anyone and everyone who will listen, they write to "experts" for advice, they talk to RV dealers, and some must dream about it—everything but make up their minds! I suspect that some of them talk the years away and go to their eternal reward never having decided anything.

My suggestion is that anyone who is seriously contemplating life on the road should set a definite time to have their minds made up— six months, a year, whatever—and at the end of that time *either go or quit thinking and talking about it.*

Always bear in mind as you're working on a decision: If you choose to go, you'll probably be embarking on a way of life that will bring you all the joys you expected—and probably a few trials and tribulations that you didn't. However, if you try it and discover later that it isn't for you, you simply reestablish a "regular" home again. But if you never make a decision at all, and instead keep thinking about it, you'll go through your retirement years always wondering what you missed.

The Maxwell Full-timing Aptitude Test

The following questions pertain to your attitudes about how you want to live your life. The objective of the test is to compare your attitudes with those most characteristic of RV fulltimers in order to determine whether or not you are suited to the full-timing lifestyle. Choose the answers that *best* describe your feelings. Mark your responses on a separate sheet of paper. Answers and scoring at end of test.

Select the answer that pops into your head first.

1. Most of the time, I
   a. am happy and completely content with my present mode of living.
   b. would like to go more, do more, and see more.
   c. feel that we live in a lousy world and there's nothing I can do about it.
2. My idea of a perfect Sunday afternoon is to
   a. sit in a comfortable chair and watch TV.
   b. work at my hobby alone.
   c. take a drive in the country on a road I've never taken before.
3 At a large gathering of people, I
   a. sometimes start conversations with strangers.
   b. find a quiet spot at which to watch from the sidelines.
   c. talk only with people I know.
4. When planning a trip, I like to
   a. choose roads I am familiar with.
   b. select roads I've never taken before.
   c. stay on the interstates when possible.
5. My spouse
   a. is my best friend.
   b. bores me much of the time.
   c. generally does what he or she likes, and I do my own thing.
6. In heavy traffic or on mountain roads, I
   a. am usually nervous or terrified.
   b. am usually bored.
   c. watch the scenery or the people in their cars.
7. When something breaks around the house or won't work, I
   a. usually try to fix it and frequently succeed.
   b. always call an expert to come and fix it.
   c. usually just let it stay broken.

8. A book that I never want to be without is
   a. a romance novel.
   b. a spy thriller.
   c. an atlas.

9. I enjoy most visiting
   a. shopping malls.
   b. historical houses.
   c. flea markets.

10. Given the choice, I would choose first to see
    a. Carlsbad Caverns.
    b. my favorite TV program.
    c. a football game.

11. My favorite food is
    a. at restaurants.
    b. what I (or my spouse) prepares.
    c. what someone else prepares.

12. My idea of the perfect way to travel is
    a. by air, staying and eating at hotels.
    b. by automobile, motels, and restaurants.
    c. by motorhome or travel trailer.

13. I would like most to see more of
    a. Europe.
    b. Asia.
    c. the United States.

14. I am happiest when I am
    a. involved in a familiar routine.
    b. embarking on a new adventure.
    c. alone in my favorite room.

15. My experience in RVing:
    a. Never done it.
    b. New at it but like it so far.
    c. Been at it for several years and love it.

16. How I feel about my home:
    a. It provides me with the roots that I must have.
    b. I love it, I am very sentimental about it, and could never give it up.
    c. It is not crucial to my happiness.
17. How I feel about my kids and grandkids:
    a. I love them, but I can leave them for extended periods of time.
    b. I have to see them every week or I am unhappy.
    c. We should all be together every Sunday and holiday.
18. Meeting new people is
    a. not very exciting or interesting.
    b. a meaningless chore most of the time.
    c. usually a pleasant experience that sometimes leads to new friends.
19. My preference in a vacation destination would be
    a. to visit relatives.
    b. Nova Scotia.
    c. a nice hotel in Chicago.
20. My spouse and I
    a. tolerate each other most of the time.
    b. often laugh at the same things.
    c. argue a lot.
21. Given the option, I would rather
    a. drive 100 miles out of the way rather than drive through Los Angeles.
    b. not drive at all if I could ride with someone else.
    c. drive over a curvy, mountain road rather than an interstate.
22. Which of these would you be least likely to leave at home on a long trip?
    a. my tool box

b. my best suit.

c. my favorite music.

23. Which would you most like to do?

    a. spend a month at a Florida beach condo.

    b. live with absolutely no work or chores.

    c. drive to Alaska.

24. Before I leave this earth, I would like most to

    a. visit all 50 states.

    b. make a lot of money.

    c. be elected to a high political office.

25. If I win the lottery, my first big purchase will be

    a. a new house.

    b. presents for all my relatives.

    c. a new motorhome or trailer.

Answers:

 1. b

 2. c

 3. a

 4. b

 5. a

 6. c

 7. a

 8. c

 9. b

10. a

11. b

12. c

13. c

14. b

15. c
16. c
17. a
18. c
19. b
20. b
21. c
22. a
23. c
24. a
25. c

Scoring:

23–25—Your chances of becoming a successful fulltimer are excellent. Pack your rig and get going.

20–22—Probably you will do okay, but you may have to work on a few problems now and then. Get more information about RVs and the lifestyle before you jump in.

15–19—Some serious questions about your success. Test the waters carefully before jumping in. Take a trial run—say for six months before cutting the home ties.

10–14—Success doubtful. You have some very anti–full-timing attitudes that will give you problems if you hit the road.

0–9—Do yourself (and others) a favor and stay at home. You'll be happier there.